JUDAISM
JUNGLE
KNIGHT
LIFE
LIGHT
MAMMAL

MATTER
MEDIA & COMMUNICATION
MEDICINE
MEDIEVAL LIFE
MESOPOTAMIA
MONET
MONEY
MUMMY

MUSIC
MYTHOLOGY
NASCAR
NATURAL DISASTERS
NORTH AMERICAN INDIAN
OCEAN
OIL
OLYMPICS

PERSPECTIVE
PHOTOGRAPHY
PIRATE
PLANT
POND & RIVER
PREHISTORIC LIFE
PRESIDENTS
PYRAMID

RELIGION
RENAISSANCE
REPTILE
RESCUE
ROBOT
ROCKS & MINERALS
RUSSIA
SEASHORE

SHAKESPEARE
SHARK
SHELL
SHIPWRECK
SKELETON
SOCCER
SPACE EXPLORATION
SPORTS

SPY
SUBMARINE
SUPER BOWL
TECHNOLOGY
TEXAS
TIME & SPACE
TITANIC
TRAIN

TREE
UNIVERSE
VAN GOGH
VIETNAM WAR
VIKING
VOLCANO & EARTHQUAKE
WATERCOLOR
WEATHER

WHALE
WILD WEST
WITCHES & MAGIC-MAKERS
WORLD SERIES
WORLD WAR I
WORLD WAR II

J. Albert Adams
Academy Media Center

Eyewitness
DINOSAUR

Thescelosaurus
skull

Iguanodon fibula
(calf bone)

Ammonite

Ornithischian
vertebra

Horsetail

Ornithischian
tail vertebra

*Zanclodon
suevicus*
snout

Redwood branch

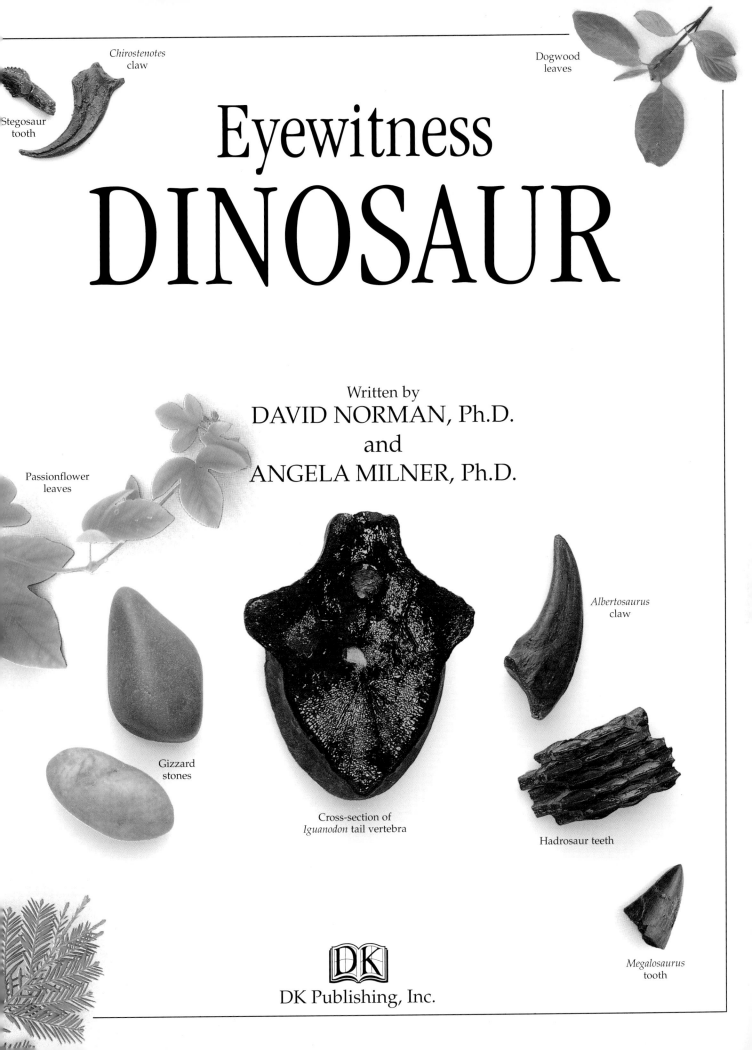

Stegosaur tooth

Chirostenotes claw

Dogwood leaves

Eyewitness
DINOSAUR

Written by
DAVID NORMAN, Ph.D.
and
ANGELA MILNER, Ph.D.

Passionflower leaves

Albertosaurus claw

Gizzard stones

Cross-section of *Iguanodon* tail vertebra

Hadrosaur teeth

Megalosaurus tooth

DK Publishing, Inc.

Hypsilophodon
vertebrae

Ginkgo
leaves

Hadrosaur
toe bone

Coelurosaur neck
vertebra

DK

LONDON, NEW YORK, MUNICH,
MELBOURNE, and DELHI

Project editor Susan McKeever
Art editor Lester Cheeseman
Senior editor Sophie Mitchell
Senior art editor Miranda Kennedy
Managing editor Sue Unstead
Managing art editor Roger Priddy
Special photography Colin Keates

REVISED EDITION
Managing editors Linda Esposito, Andrew Macintyre
Managing art editor Jane Thomas
Category publisher Linda Martin
Art director Simon Webb
Editor Clare Hibbert
Reference compiler Sue Nicholson
Art editors Andrew Nash, Joanna Pocock
Consultants Michael Benton, Dougal Dixon
Production Jenny Jacoby
Picture research Celia Dearing
DTP designer Siu Yin Ho

U.S. editor Elizabeth Hester
Senior editor Beth Sutinis
Art editor Dirk Kaufman
U.S. production Chris Avgherinos
U.S. DTP designer Milos Orlovic

This Eyewitness ® Guide has been conceived by
Dorling Kindersley Limited and Editions Gallimard

This edition first published in the United States in 2004
by DK Publishing, Inc., 375 Hudson Street, New York, NY 10014

07 08 10 9 8 7 6 5 4

Copyright © 1989, © 2004, Dorling Kindersley Limited

A catalog record for this book is available from the Library of Congress.
ISBN 13: 978-0-7566-0647-3 (PLC)
ISBN 13: 978-0-7566-0665-7 (ALB)

Color reproduction by Colourscan, Singapore
Printed in China by Toppan Printing Co., (Shenzhen) Ltd.

Dryosaurus femur
(thigh bone)

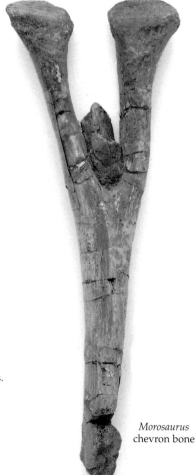

Morosaurus
chevron bone

Ornithomimus
toe

Monkey puzzle
branch

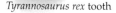

Tyrannosaurus rex tooth

Discover more at
www.dk.com

Contents

Heterodontosaurus skull

What were the dinosaurs?

BACK IN THE MISTS OF TIME, there lived an extraordinary group of animals called dinosaurs. They survived for nearly 150 million years, and then disappeared off the face of the Earth in the most mysterious extinction ever. Many of them were gigantic, and some were no bigger than a chicken. Some were peaceful and ate only plants; others were fierce sharp-toothed flesh eaters. Dinosaurs were reptiles, just like the living iguana lizard on this page. They had scaly skin and laid eggs. But unlike the lizard, which has short, sprawling legs, dinosaurs had long legs tucked under their bodies, which meant that they could move much more efficiently. Many other reptiles shared the dinosaur world, swimming in the sea and flying in the air, but dinosaurs lived only on land. We know about them today because their bones and teeth have been preserved in rock as fossils.

HIPS CAN TELL A STORY
Dinosaurs fall into two main groups, according to the structure of their hipbones. Saurischian, or "lizard-hipped" dinosaurs, had hips in which the two lower bones pointed in opposite directions. Ornithischian, or "bird-hipped" dinosaurs, had the two lower hipbones lying together behind the back leg.

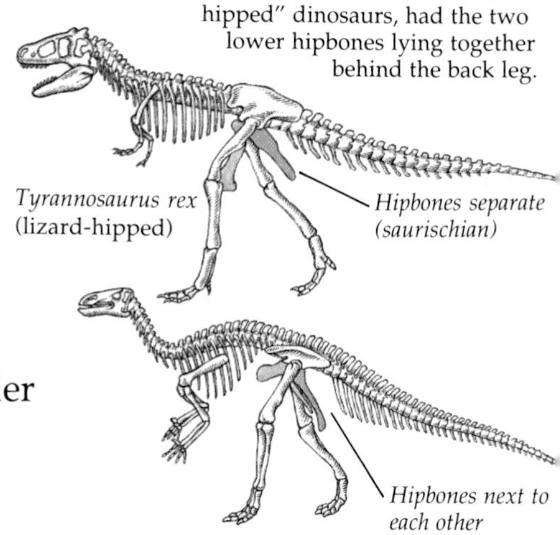

Tyrannosaurus rex
(lizard-hipped)

*Hipbones separate
(saurischian)*

Iguanodon
(bird-hipped)

*Hipbones next to
each other
(ornithischian)*

Iguana lizard

DINOSAURS COULDN'T FLY!
Flying reptiles, like the pterosaurs shown here feeding on a *Triceratops* carcass, shared the dinosaur world, but were not dinosaurs. No dinosaur could fly.

Sharp claws

Characteristic scaly skin

Dinosaurs may have been this color

Nostril

LIVING DINOSAUR?

The tuatara is a rare, endangered species of lizard found only on islands off the coast of New Zealand. Extinct relatives of the tuatara lived during the dinosaur age. The spines on its back look a little like some dinosaurs' back spines.

HOW DINOSAURS EVOLVED

The nearest living reptile relatives of dinosaurs are crocodiles. Millions of years ago, an ancient crocodile-like ancestor, or thecodont ("socket-toothed reptile"), developed the habit of running on land. Over millions of years thecodonts changed the way they moved their legs, became smaller and faster, and eventually evolved into the earliest dinosaurs.

IN THE WATER
Proterosuchus was an early thecodont that spent most of its time in the water.

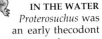

ON FOUR LEGS
Thecodonts like *Euparkeria* left the water to live on land, walking on all fours.

"BIRD CROCODILE"
Ornithosuchus was a later, predatory thecodont that walked on two legs - a cousin of the first dinosaurs.

UPRIGHT AND DANGEROUS
Staurikosaurus, a flesh eater, was one of the earliest dinosaurs. Its fully upright gait made it a fast mover, giving it an advantage over the thecodonts before it.

Neck frill

WHAT'S LEFT. . .

One of the earliest dinosaurs to be discovered was named after an iguana (pp. 8-9). This scaly green iguana looks prehistoric, and indeed has features in common with some dinosaurs, like sharp claws and the texture of the skin.

Short, sprawling legs

Early discoveries

DINOSAUR MAN
This cartoon shows Sir Richard Owen, the man who coined the name dinosaur. He is sitting astride a giant ground sloth (a fossil mammal that was found in South America).

Iguanodon tooth from lower jaw

Aᴌᴛʜᴏᴜɢʜ ᴅɪɴᴏsᴀᴜʀ remains have been around for millions of years, people knew nothing about these extraordinary creatures until the 19th century. One of the first people to discover dinosaur bones was an English doctor named Gideon Mantell, who collected rocks and fossils as a hobby. In 1820, Dr. Mantell, with his wife Mary Ann, found some large teeth embedded in stone. Mantell had never seen teeth quite like them before, and when he found some bones nearby, he began to do some serious research into the find. After a lot of work, Dr. Mantell concluded that the teeth and bones had belonged to some kind of giant reptile, which he named *Iguanodon*, meaning "Iguana tooth" (pp. 6-7). Two more giant reptiles were soon discovered in Great Britain and named *Megalosaurus* and *Hylaeosaurus*. But it was not until 1841 that these creatures were given a group name. An eminent scientist of the time, Richard Owen, declared that they should be called "dinosaurs," meaning "terrible lizards." Thus began an exciting time of discovery in the scientific world. The great dinosaur hunt was on.

Worn edge

Tooth from upper jaw

THE FIRST TEETH
Still embedded in the gritty stone in which they were found by the Mantells are the original *Iguanodon* teeth. The top edges of the dinosaur teeth were worn down by the plants it chewed. (pp. 26-27).

Horn on nose was actually a thumb spike

Long whiplash tail like an iguana lizard

A ROUGH SKETCH
Dr. Mantell had discovered a collection of bones and teeth. But what on earth had the owner of the bones looked like when it was alive? Mantell pictured it as a gigantic lizard, a bit like an iguana. He drew a picture of it perched on a branch, with its thumb spike (of which he had found only one) placed on its nose

IGUANODON

Gideon Mantell's original drawing of *Iguanodon*

Part of an *Iguanodon* backbone

Backbones fused together

THE DISCOVERER
Although he was a medical doctor by profession, Gideon Mantell was an enthusiastic collector of rocks and fossils. As his collection grew, his home began to look like a museum.

DINNER IN A DINOSAUR
As the interest in dinosaurs grew, a great display of giant models was mounted in the gardens of London's Crystal Palace. Before the *Iguanodon* model was finished, the sculptor held a dinner party for 20 people inside it.

MORE BONES
More bones from *Iguanodon* found by Gideon Mantell include this portion of the backbone which fitted between the hips of the animal.

Iguanodon tibia (shinbone)

MONSTERS IN THE PARK
These two concrete models of *Iguanodon* were made by the sculptor Benjamin Waterhouse Hawkins in the last century. Although inaccurate - *Iguanodon* looked nothing like this (p. 39) - they can be seen to this day in the park at the Crystal Palace, London.

Dinosaur landscape

Dinosaurs LIVED on Earth for nearly 150 million years, and it is not surprising that their world changed substantially during this time. Continents, at first just one great landmass, gradually drifted apart until they resembled the modern arrangement that we are familiar with. This meant that the climate changed as well, and both these factors influenced the types of plants that grew. These changes happened slowly over millions of years and animals adapted accordingly. At the beginning of the dinosaur age, the landscape was covered with low shrubby fern-like plants. Then came a time when huge evergreen forests and groves of cycads flourished. Later on, the first flowering plants added color to the scene. Many plants and flowers that the dinosaurs may have eaten can still be seen growing today.

ANCIENT PUZZLE
Living monkey puzzle trees are relatives of ones which grew long before dinosaurs ever walked the Earth.

FIR FEAST
Herbivorous dinosaurs had enough vegetation to satisfy their appetites. Duckbilled dinosaurs, such as *Parasaurolophus*, above, could cope with tough plants because their jaws and teeth were so powerful. Even fir needles posed no problem.

CYCAD FROND
Cycads were abundant during most of the dinosaur reign, and, though very rare, can still be found today.

A DINOSAUR HOME
This scene shows the type of landscape that would have been familiar to dinosaurs of about 130 million years ago. Horsetails, ferns, and cycads are everywhere.

Conifer:
Pseudotsuga menziesii

Passionflower:
Passiflora sp.

Holly:
Ilex aquifolium

Cycad:
Cycas revoluta

THE FLOWERING
The first flowering plant appeared
during the last period of the dinosaurs'
reign. Flowering plants can reproduce more
quickly than other types, and they rapidly
came to dominate plant communities
worldwide. Flowers introduced color
and variety into the diets of
dinosaurs .

Ginkgo:
Ginkgo biloba

English Laurel:
Prunus laurocerasus
"Otto Luykeres"

A MAGNOLIA
It is surprising to
think of dinosaurs
eating flowers, but
when magnolias
appeared about
100 million years
ago, they were no doubt
munched upon by many
plant-eating dinosaurs.

Magnolia:
Magnolia loebneri

Fern:
Marattia werneri

Fern:
chnum sp.

Horsetail:
*Equisetum
giganteum*

Dogwood:
Cornus alba

Little and large

A LOT OF PEOPLE think of dinosaurs as being massive creatures, big enough to reach the treetops, but there were also tiny dinosaurs, ones that would not even reach your knee. The biggest creatures ever to walk the Earth were the sauropod group of dinosaurs, which were all plant-eaters. For a long time, *Brachiosaurus* was the biggest sauropod that we knew much about. Weighing about 70 tons, it was 70 ft (22 m) long, and stood 39 ft (12 m) high - about as tall as a four-story building. But now bones have been found belonging to even larger dinosaurs. *Paralititan*, found in Africa, was about the same weight as *Brachiosaurus* but could have been up to 100 ft (30 m) long. *Argentinosaurus*, found in South America, was around 130 ft (40 m) long and probably weighed as much as 20 large elephants. By contrast with these quite peaceful giants, the tiny dinosaurs like *Compsognathus* (far right) were mostly agile, crafty meat-eaters, some no heavier than a cat.

AS TALL AS A HOUSE
This French engraving shows a popular image of dinosaurs as giants: an alarming visitor to a Paris street investigates a balcony on the fifth floor of a tall building.

THE OWNER OF THE BONE
This *Brachiosaurus* is the type of dinosaur that owned the massive leg bone (far right). The huge, pillar-like forelimbs were longer than the hindlimbs - probably to help it to reach up to the treetops for food.

FANTASTIC FEMUR
The femur (upper leg bone) shown at right belonged to a *Brachiosaurus*. If you stood next to a *Brachiosaurus* leg, you would hardly reach past its knee bone! The gentleman (left) is examining an *Apatosaurus* femur, which measures 6 ft 10 in (2.1 m) long. *Apatosaurus* was another type of sauropod dinosaur.

Part of a large *Brachiosaurus* femur, ending in knee joint

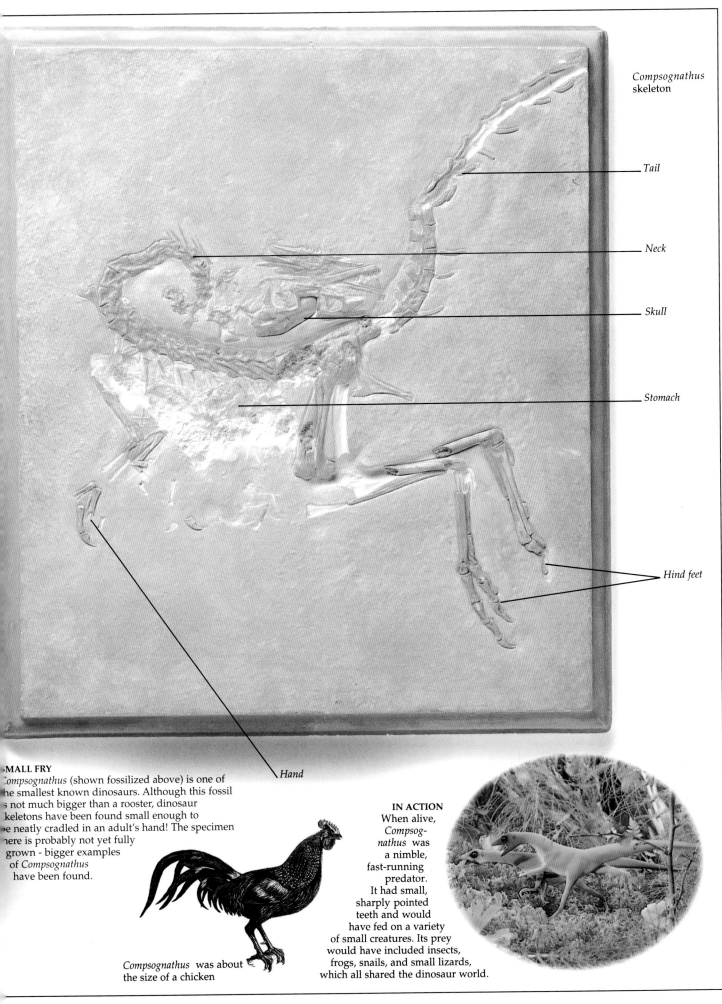

Compsognathus
skeleton

Tail

Neck

Skull

Stomach

Hind feet

Hand

SMALL FRY
Compsognathus (shown fossilized above) is one of the smallest known dinosaurs. Although this fossil is not much bigger than a rooster, dinosaur skeletons have been found small enough to be neatly cradled in an adult's hand! The specimen here is probably not yet fully grown - bigger examples of *Compsognathus* have been found.

Compsognathus was about the size of a chicken

IN ACTION
When alive, *Compsognathus* was a nimble, fast-running predator. It had small, sharply pointed teeth and would have fed on a variety of small creatures. Its prey would have included insects, frogs, snails, and small lizards, which all shared the dinosaur world.

The long-necked beast

Small skull compared to size of body

THE MASSIVE CREATURE that can be seen spread across the next eight pages was one of the biggest dinosaurs ever to walk the Earth. It was called *Diplodocus*, and like *Brachiosaurus*, below, it belonged to a group of dinosaurs called sauropods (p. 12). *Diplodocus* looked extraordinary, with its long neck and tail, and a head that was tiny in proportion to the rest of its body. This type of body suited its lifestyle perfectly. It could reach up to feed at the tops of the very tall trees, like conifers, that grew at the time. Its small head allowed it to browse among the vegetation, where few other dinosaurs could reach. This type of feeding needed a special type of neck – one that was strong, light, and flexible, in order to be raised and lowered easily. Having stripped one area bare of food, it would have ambled off with its companions in search of new feeding grounds. If *Diplodocus* was threatened by a meat-eater, its only defense would have been its bulk, and its long, whip-like tail (pp. 20-21).

NECK SUPPORT
This head and neck belong to *Brachiosaurus*. Like *Diplodocus*, it must have had powerful neck muscles that could raise its head. It would also have needed a strong heart to pump blood at high pressure so that it could reach the brain.

SHORT AND FLEXIBLE
Unlike *Diplodocus*, a predator such as *Tyrannosaurus rex* (left) needed a neck that was short, powerful, and flexible. It had to be short to support the large head. Flexibility in the neck meant that *Tyrannosaurus rex* could twist its head around to wrench flesh from its prey.

A HARD NECK
Triceratops' neck (left) needed to be short and extremely strong in order to support the weight of its head, which it used to tear off tough vegetation. It also fought and charged enemies with its three fearsome horns (pp. 30-31).

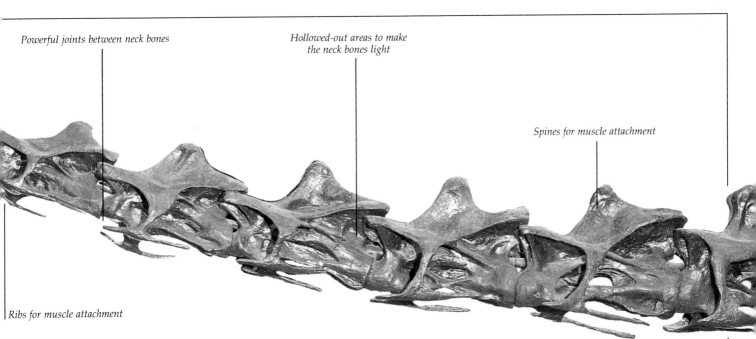

Powerful joints between neck bones

Hollowed-out areas to make the neck bones light

Spines for muscle attachment

Ribs for muscle attachment

JURASSIC BROWSERS

Due to its enormous size, *Brachiosaurus* must have spent most of its time eating. Traveling as part of a herd, the dinosaur would have fed in riverside forests and open woodland containing conifers, cycads, and ferns. Its fossil remains have been found in Africa, Europe, and North America. By swinging its long neck, *Brachiosaurus* could reach the leaves of tall trees. Lowering it, the dinosaur could nibble at low-growing ferns.

The beast continues. . .

CRANING THE NECK

The design of a *Diplodocus* neck is rather like that of a human-made crane. The jib, which juts out from the main tower and from which the hooks used for lifting things are suspended, is like the dinosaur's neck. The heavy base of the crane, which keeps it from toppling over, is like *Diplodocus'* sturdy body. The jib of a crane has to be light and strong, so the engineer builds it with a light metal framework. *Diplodocus* had lightweight but very strong bones in its neck, which it could raise and lower just like the jib of a crane.

Neck bone

The backbone story

The body of *Diplodocus* was designed to bear and move enormous weight, and the backbone, between shoulders and hips, was the powerhouse of the whole animal. The back bones (vertebrae) had to be strong enough to support the enormous weight of the neck, tail, and belly. However, they were hollowed out for lightness. Narrow spines, pointing upward from the top of the backbone, acted as anchor points for powerful back muscles. Long ribs pointing downward curved around the belly and helped to hold the backbone in position against the great weight of the belly. They also protected the internal organs of the animal.

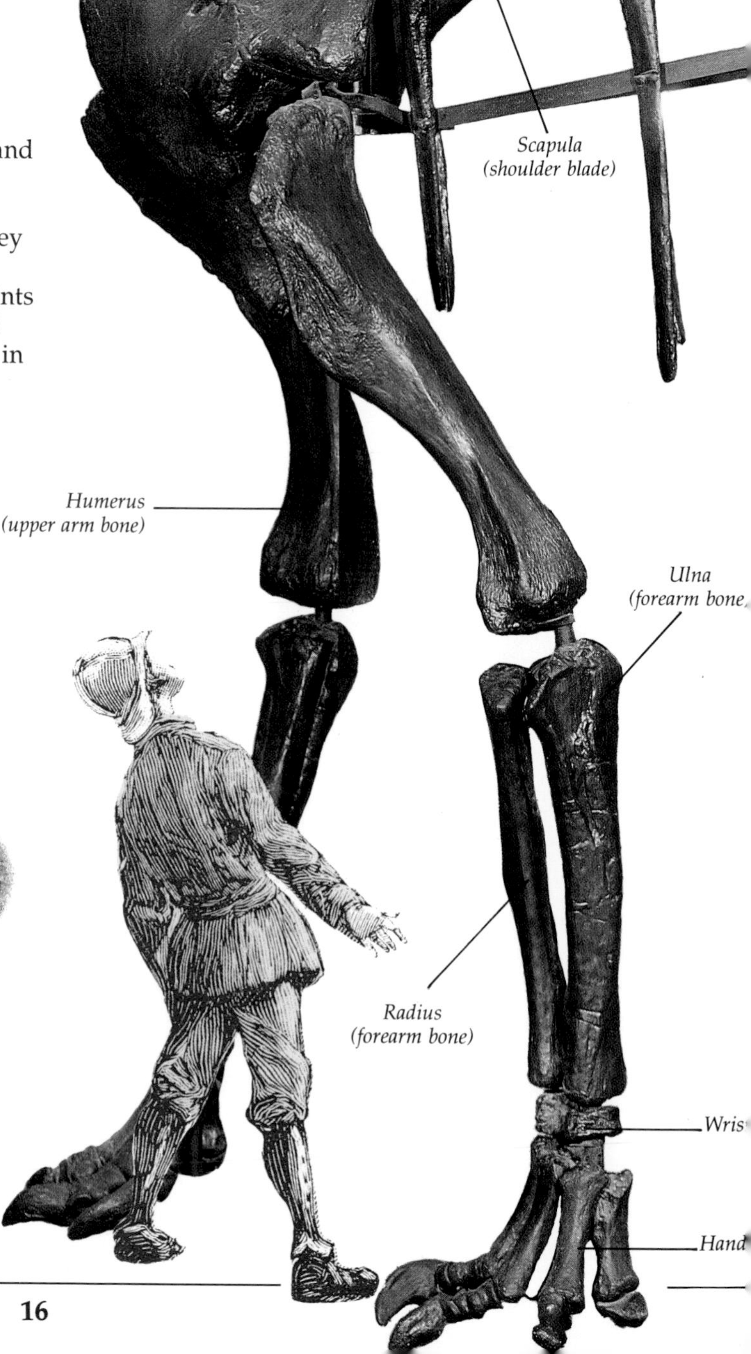

Scapula
(shoulder blade)

Humerus
(upper arm bone)

Ulna
(forearm bone)

Temple of Jupiter,
Athens

Radius
(forearm bone)

LEGS LIKE PILLARS
The strong legs of *Diplodocus* supported
its body just as the pillars of this Greek
temple support the heavy stone roof.
The limb bones were heavy and dense,
capable of holding up the enormous
weight of the dinosaur's body.

Wris

Hand

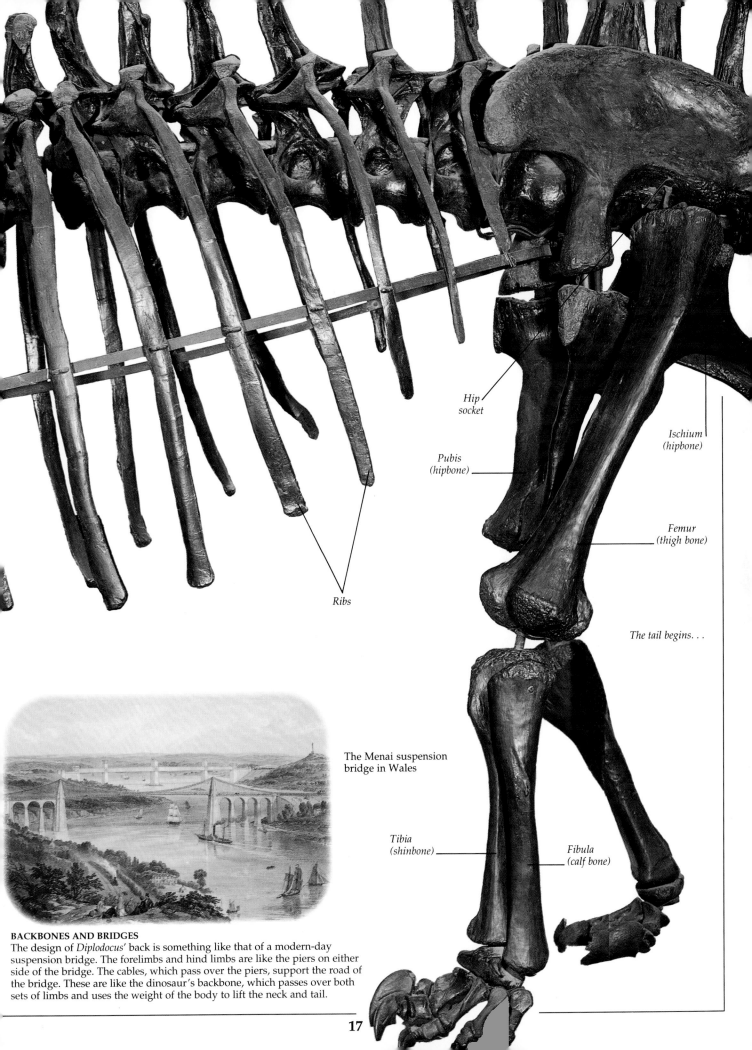

Hip
socket

Ischium
(hipbone)

Pubis
(hipbone)

Femur
(thigh bone)

Ribs

The tail begins. . .

The Menai suspension
bridge in Wales

Tibia
(shinbone)

Fibula
(calf bone)

BACKBONES AND BRIDGES
The design of *Diplodocus'* back is something like that of a modern-day
suspension bridge. The forelimbs and hind limbs are like the piers on either
side of the bridge. The cables, which pass over the piers, support the road of
the bridge. These are like the dinosaur's backbone, which passes over both
sets of limbs and uses the weight of the body to lift the neck and tail.

Kangaroos sometimes rest or groom
themselves while sitting on their
hind legs, using the tail as a
balancing aid. They also
balance on their tails while
fighting. Leaning only on
the tail, they can kick out
with their feet, as in this
picture. They do not
usually wear boxing
gloves, however!

Kangaroo and boxer
engaged in combat

*Ischium
(hip bone)*

Elongated chevron

All about tails

Tails can have a surprising number of uses.
The most important one for living reptiles, as well
as dinosaurs, is that it provides an anchor point for the
attachment of large leg-moving muscles, running from the
sides of the tail bones to the top of the hind leg. Sauropod
dinosaurs such as *Diplodocus* may have used their tails for balancing. By
rearing up and balancing on hind legs and tail, they would have extended
their reach into the treetops,
perhaps gaining access
to better-quality food. Fast-
moving two-legged dinosaurs
used their tails to balance
while running.

*Chevron bones become
more flattened towards
the middle of the tail*

*Diplodocus rearing up on its
hind legs to feed*

BALANCING ACT
Until recently, scientists believed
that sauropods could only walk
on all fours. But experts who have
studied the size and strength of the
legs, and the tail structure, agree
that sauropods often reared up
on their hind legs to feed.

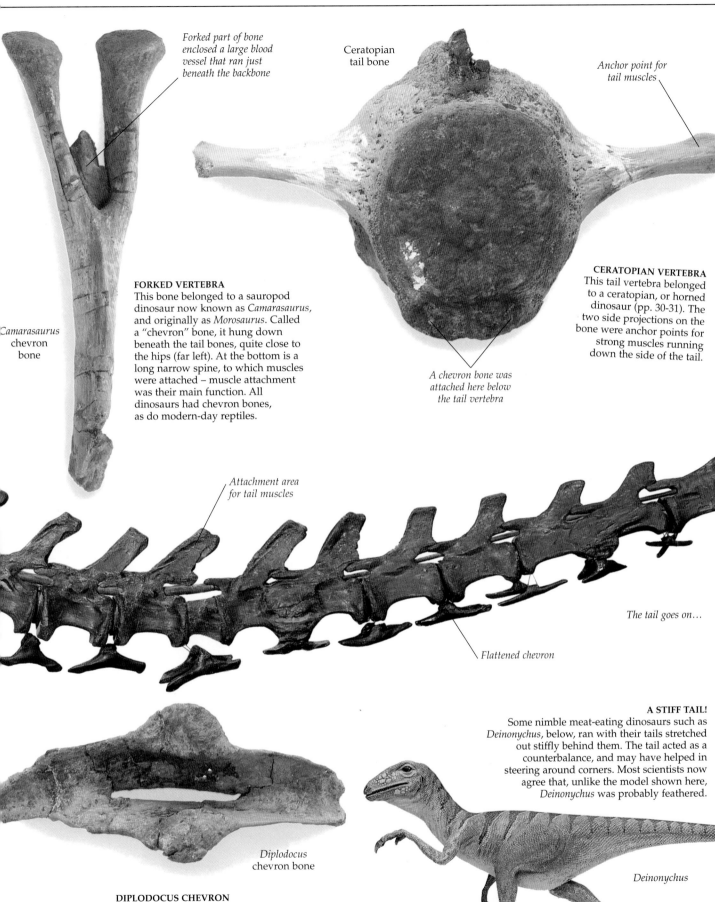

Forked part of bone
enclosed a large blood
vessel that ran just
beneath the backbone

Ceratopian
tail bone

Anchor point for
tail muscles

Camarasaurus
chevron
bone

FORKED VERTEBRA
This bone belonged to a sauropod
dinosaur now known as *Camarasaurus*,
and originally as *Morosaurus*. Called
a "chevron" bone, it hung down
beneath the tail bones, quite close to
the hips (far left). At the bottom is a
long narrow spine, to which muscles
were attached – muscle attachment
was their main function. All
dinosaurs had chevron bones,
as do modern-day reptiles.

CERATOPIAN VERTEBRA
This tail vertebra belonged
to a ceratopian, or horned
dinosaur (pp. 30-31). The
two side projections on the
bone were anchor points for
strong muscles running
down the side of the tail.

A chevron bone was
attached here below
the tail vertebra

Attachment area
for tail muscles

The tail goes on…

Flattened chevron

A STIFF TAIL!
Some nimble meat-eating dinosaurs such as
Deinonychus, below, ran with their tails stretched
out stiffly behind them. The tail acted as a
counterbalance, and may have helped in
steering around corners. Most scientists now
agree that, unlike the model shown here,
Deinonychus was probably feathered.

Diplodocus
chevron bone

Deinonychus

DIPLODOCUS CHEVRON
Toward the middle of *Diplodocus'* tail, the chevron bones
became more flattened and boat-shaped, like this one,
photographed from above. These types of chevron bones
may have acted as skids to protect the underside of the tail
as it dragged along the ground.

The tale of defense

TAILS WERE A VERY USEFUL MEANS of defense for many plant-eating dinosaurs, and what they lacked in teeth and claws was compensated for by their ingenious tails. Some dinosaurs, like the sauropods, had long, thin tails, which they used as whiplashes. Apart from their daunting size, this was their main form of defense. Armored dinosaurs, or ankylosaurs, had bony clubs on their tails, as well as being protected from head to toe with body armor. Stegosaurs, or plated dinosaurs (pp. 34-35), sported formidable sharp tail spikes, which they used to lash out at attackers. Some modern-day reptiles use their tails in self-defense: crocodiles will lash out at an enemy with their heavy, scale-covered tails, and many lizards have long whiplash-type tails. No living reptiles, however, have defensive tails with attachments as spectacular as the terrifying spikes and clubs used by some dinosaurs to defend themselves.

WALKING THORN BUSH
This armored dinosaur, *Gastonia*, was the length of a large car. Unlike fellow ankylosaur *Euoplocephalus* (below right), *Gastonia* did not have a heavy tail club. However, big spines could have made its tail a formidable weapon. The rest of *Gastonia*'s body was also studded with sharp, defensive spines.

Tail bones

Joint between tail bones

Tail bones become narrower towards the end

Bony studs

Scelidosaurus

Long muscular tail

USEFUL TAIL
Scelidosaurus was a plant eater that relied mostly on its armored skin to protect it from predators. But its long tail may have given it an extra advantage. It could have used it to balance while it reared up on hind legs in order to run away from a pursuing meat eater.

THORNY DEVIL
Some living reptiles, like the Moloch lizard, above, are so well armored from head to toe that they don't need a special defensive tail. Few predators would attempt an attack on this spiky lizard. It lives in dry or desert areas of Australia.

Some lethal tails

All the dinosaurs that used their tails in defense were four-footed and herbivorous (p. 26). Those dinosaurs that walked on two legs, like the duckbills (p. 28) needed their tails to balance, so they had no clubs or spikes. They had to rely on speed or camouflage for defense. The whiplash used by some sauropods, like *Diplodocus*, would have annoyed large meat eaters, and probably caused quite a stinging pain. The fearsome-looking clubs and spikes belonging to the ankylosaurs and stegosaurs were often used as a silent threat – rather like saying, "Don't come any closer!"

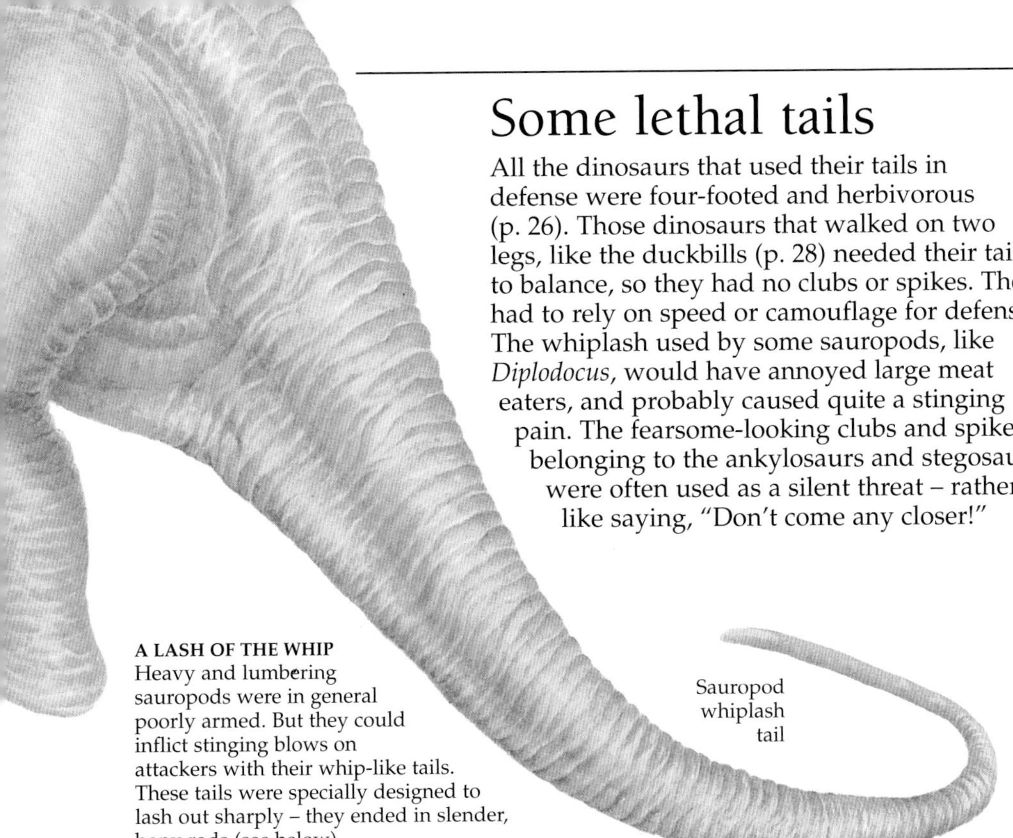

Stegosaurus tail spike

A LASH OF THE WHIP
Heavy and lumbering sauropods were in general poorly armed. But they could inflict stinging blows on attackers with their whip-like tails. These tails were specially designed to lash out sharply – they ended in slender, bony rods (see below).

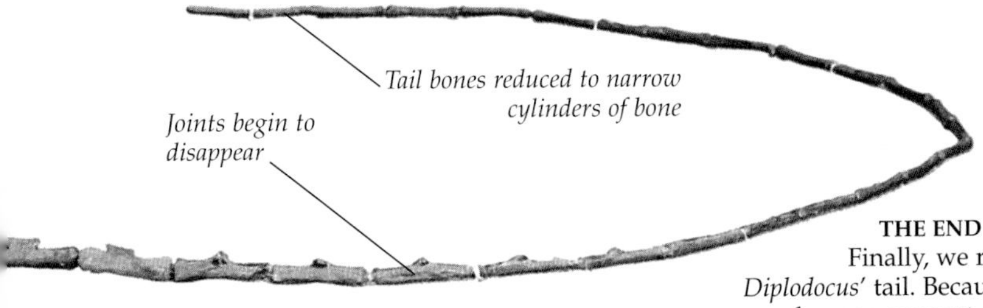

Sauropod whiplash tail

Rough area for attachment of horny covering

Tail bones reduced to narrow cylinders of bone

Joints begin to disappear

THE END OF THE TAIL
Finally, we reach the end of *Diplodocus'* tail. Because they did not have to support any muscle, the bones at the tip have become narrow cylinders. This also makes the tail into an effective whiplash.

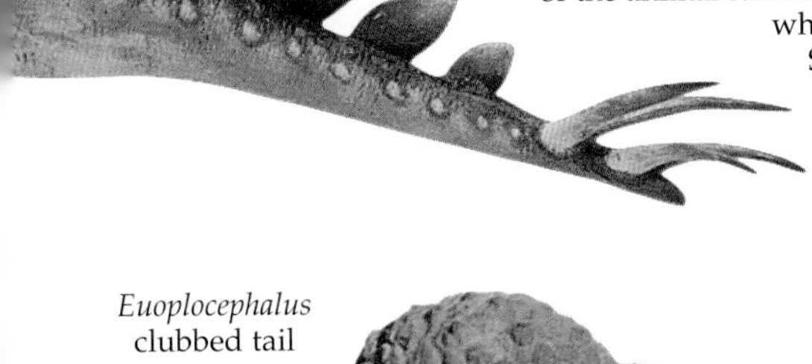

Stegosaurus spiked tail

Sharp defensive spikes

A SPIKY TAIL
This is what the tail spikes of *Stegosaurus* would have looked like when attached. The bony plates of the animal ran down the tail to meet the spikes, which were confined to the tip. So when the tail was swished to the side, the tip was the part that moved fastest, causing the most damage.

Euoplocephalus clubbed tail

CLUBBED TAIL
This armored dinosaur's tail ended in a huge, heavy, bony club. This was made out of several chunks of bone, all welded together into a single lump. The club sometimes measured as much as 3 ft (1 m) across. The dinosaur, called *Euoplocephalus*, would have needed very powerful and flexible tail muscles in order to swing such a tail around and to drive the club into an enemy.

SPIKE STORY
Shown here at half life-size, this *Stegosaurus* tail spike (pp. 34-35) would have been covered by a tough layer of horn in life, and sharply pointed at the end. Swung against the soft underbelly of a meat eater, it would have inflicted a terrible, crippling wound.

Dinosaur diets

BY THE RIVER
This early-20th-century illustration depicts a scene from 190 million years ago, with meat-eating dinosaurs, swimming reptiles, and flying pterosaurs all sharing the same landscape. But although these creatures did all exist at that time, it is unlikely that prehistoric reptiles would have thronged together in this way.

MANY OF US IMAGINE DINOSAURS as being fearsome meat-eating creatures. But some were peaceful plant-eaters that simply browsed among the treetops, tearing off leaves. Other dinosaurs were able to eat a mixed diet of meat and plants, as humans do. Those that were not vegetarian did not confine themselves to dinosaur meat. They would have eaten anything that moved, including insects and birds. Fossilized dinosaur remains can tell us a lot about what the animal ate when it was alive. The most important clues are to be found in the shape and arrangement of the jaws and teeth. Even the overall shape of a dinosaur's body tells a story – meat-eaters often had big heads and short, powerful necks in order to wrench lumps of meat off a kill. The long necks of many plant eaters were useful for reaching up to the treetops to feed.

VEGETARIAN SKULL
This skull belonged to a huge plant-eater, or herbivore, called *Diplodocus*. All of the thin, pencil-like teeth are at the front of the mouth. *Diplodocus* would have used them like a rake to draw in fern leaves and other vegetation. Unable to chew, *Diplodocus* simply swallowed what it raked in.

*Orbit
(eye socket)*

Pencil-like teeth

*Weak
lower
jaw*

Diplodocus skull

SERIOUS TEETH

The fearsome rows of curved, serrated (sawlike) teeth in the *Allosaurus* skull (below) are typical of carnivores (meat eaters). The "windows" in the massive skull helped to reduce its weight. *Allosaurus* may have fed on the young of herbivores such as *Diplodocus* (opposite). An adult *Diplodocus* would have been too big to tackle, unless *Allosaurus* hunted in packs.

Large cavity in front of eye for jaw muscles

Orbit (eye socket)

Large serrated teeth

Allosaurus skull

Powerful lower jaw

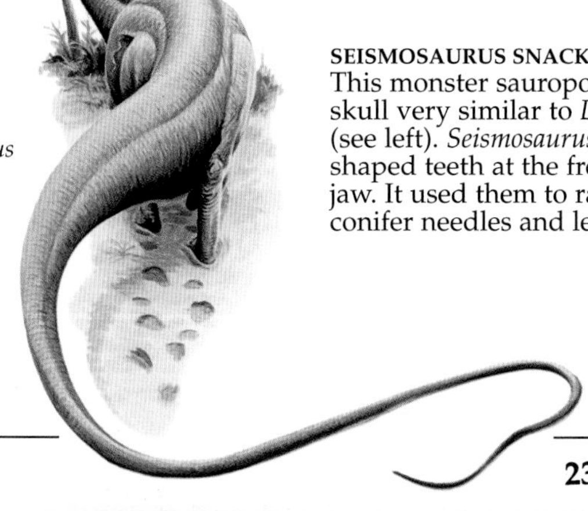

Seismosaurus

SEISMOSAURUS SNACK

This monster sauropod had a skull very similar to *Diplodocus'* (see left). *Seismosaurus* had peg-shaped teeth at the front of its jaw. It used them to rake in conifer needles and leaves.

Massospondylus skull (below)

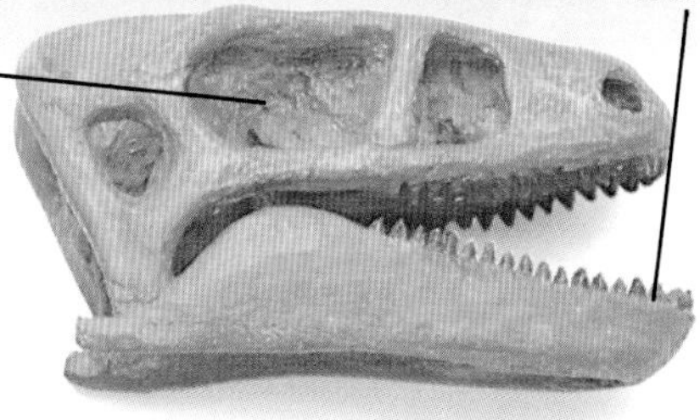

Small coarse teeth

Orbit (eye socket)

DUAL-DIET DINOSAUR

The skull above belonged to a *Massospondylus*. Its small, coarse-edged teeth were multi-purpose - they could chew either meat or plants. Animals who can eat like this are called omnivores.

Meat eaters

ALL THE MEAT-EATING DINOSAURS belonged to a group called Theropoda, which means "beast footed." Some of the meat-eating dinosaurs were called carnosaurs or "flesh lizards" - large animals with big heads, powerful legs, and short arms. Like all theropods, they walked on two legs, probably not very fast because of the bulk they had to carry. They had big heads which held long jaws lined with huge curved teeth, serrated like steak knives. Carnosaurs pursued and ate other dinosaurs, and also fed on dead animals that they found. They would kill their prey with the help of their clawed feet and then tear off the flesh of the victim with their hands and teeth. Their hands were also well-equipped with sharp claws. The other meat eaters were known as coelurosaurs, or "hollow-tailed lizards." Coelurosaurs were lightly built, nimble creatures with long grasping arms and hands and long, narrow jaws. They could run very fast and could catch small mammals and insects. After a carnosaur had eaten its fill, a coelurosaur would often move in to eat the leftover scraps.

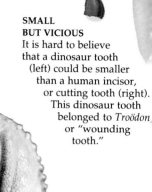

SMALL BUT VICIOUS
It is hard to believe that a dinosaur tooth (left) could be smaller than a human incisor, or cutting tooth (right). This dinosaur tooth belonged to *Troödon* or "wounding tooth."

The king

Tyrannosaurus rex is probably the best known (and most feared) of the carnosaurs. A formidable 39 ft (12 m) long, it had a massive skull with powerful jaws that held serrated teeth up to 7 in (18 cm) long. It probably used its tiny arms to push itself upright after it had been lying down.

Backward-curving teeth gave carnosaurs a better grip on a victim

Albertosaurus lower jaw

NUTHETES TOOTH
Still embedded in rock, this tooth came from a small meat eater called *Nuthetes*.

SMALLER GNASHER
Not all tyrannosaur teeth were huge. This small one is curved, in order to hook into its victim.

LION'S SLICER
Meat-eating animals, like lions, have developed special slicing teeth. No dinosaur had a tooth like this.

The large, curved tooth of *Megalosaurus*

Fine serrations like those on a steak knife

NEW GNASHER
Meat-eating dinosaurs' teeth kept growing and were constantly replaced throughout life. This megalosaur tooth is a "new" one.

Cracks which occurred during fossilization

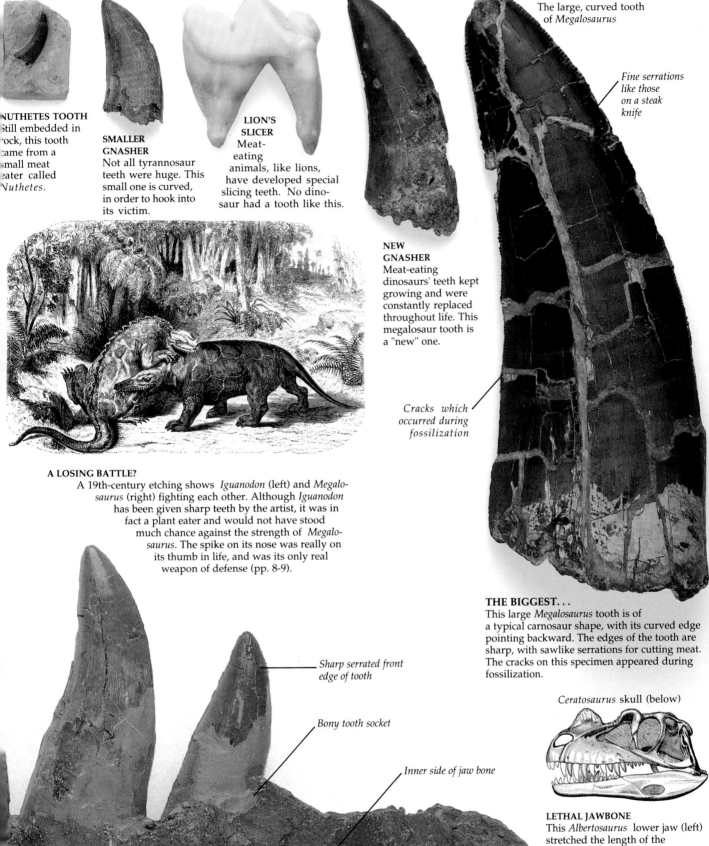

A LOSING BATTLE?
A 19th-century etching shows *Iguanodon* (left) and *Megalosaurus* (right) fighting each other. Although *Iguanodon* has been given sharp teeth by the artist, it was in fact a plant eater and would not have stood much chance against the strength of *Megalosaurus*. The spike on its nose was really on its thumb in life, and was its only real weapon of defense (pp. 8-9).

THE BIGGEST. . .
This large *Megalosaurus* tooth is of a typical carnosaur shape, with its curved edge pointing backward. The edges of the tooth are sharp, with sawlike serrations for cutting meat. The cracks on this specimen appeared during fossilization.

Ceratosaurus skull (below)

Sharp serrated front edge of tooth

Bony tooth socket

Inner side of jaw bone

LETHAL JAWBONE
This *Albertosaurus* lower jaw (left) stretched the length of the animal's skull. Powerful jaw muscles, reaching up behind the eye, were attached to the area without teeth. These would have produced a powerful bite, snapping the jaw shut on impact with its prey. The skull above, which belonged to another carnosaur, shows the same basic design.

Plant eaters

MANY OF THE DINOSAURS were plant eaters, including the biggest of all, the sauropods (pp. 12-13). Eating a diet of plants causes animals many more problems than eating meat. Plants are made of tough materials like cellulose and woody lignin and need to be broken down before digestion can take place in the animal's stomach. Plant-eating dinosaurs coped with their diet in a variety of ways: the sauropods did not chew at all, but simply swallowed raked-in vegetation. This passed directly to the stomach and was ground up by deliberately swallowed gastroliths, or "gizzard stones," or was fermented by bacteria, as in a cow's stomach. The hadrosaurs, or duckbilled dinosaurs, had special teeth which ground and chopped their food before they swallowed it. Ceratopsians tackled tough plants with their extra-strong jaws and scissor-like teeth. All of the bird-hipped dinosaurs (p. 6) were plant eaters.

Plant-eating dinosaurs would have eaten evergreens such as this yew leaf

TINY TEETH
This jaw came from *Echinodon*, one of the smallest plant-eating dinosaurs. The tiny teeth had spiked edges, like those of an iguana lizard, which eats a mixed diet of plants and meat.

Main jawbone

Ceratopsian beak

SCISSOR TOOTH
This tooth came from a ceratopsian dinosaur, like *Triceratops* (below). After tearing off the vegetation with its beak (far left), it would then have sliced it up with its sharp teeth.

Notch for replacement tooth to grow into

Cycad plant

TOUGH AND STRINGY
Some experts believe that ceratopsian dinosaurs evolved specially enabling them to eat new kinds of tough plants. They would have eaten the leaves of palmlike cycads (left), and maybe even tackled pine cones (above).

Pine cone

BUILT TO CHEW
Dinosaurs like this *Triceratops* (pp. 30-31) ate tough, fibrous plants (above). *Triceratops*, like many ceratopsians, had extremely powerful jaws and sharp teeth that helped it tear out and eat these plants.

CROPPING BEAK
A beak like this ceratopsian one (p. 30) was ideal for cropping tough plants. The rough grooves and pits mark the place where the horny covering of keratin was attached. The lower, wider part of the bone (called the predentary) fitted tightly against the lower jaw.

THE GREATEST GRINDER

Duckbilled dinosaurs had the most spectacular array of teeth of any plant-eating dinosaur. Hundreds of sharp, diamond-shaped teeth lined both sides of their upper and lower jaws. The teeth were set way back in the jaw, which left the broad beak toothless. The grinding surface formed by these teeth acted like a vegetable grater to shred the plants. New teeth constantly grew to replace the worn ones, as can be seen here, pushing up the top layer of teeth in this *Edmontosaurus* jaw (below).

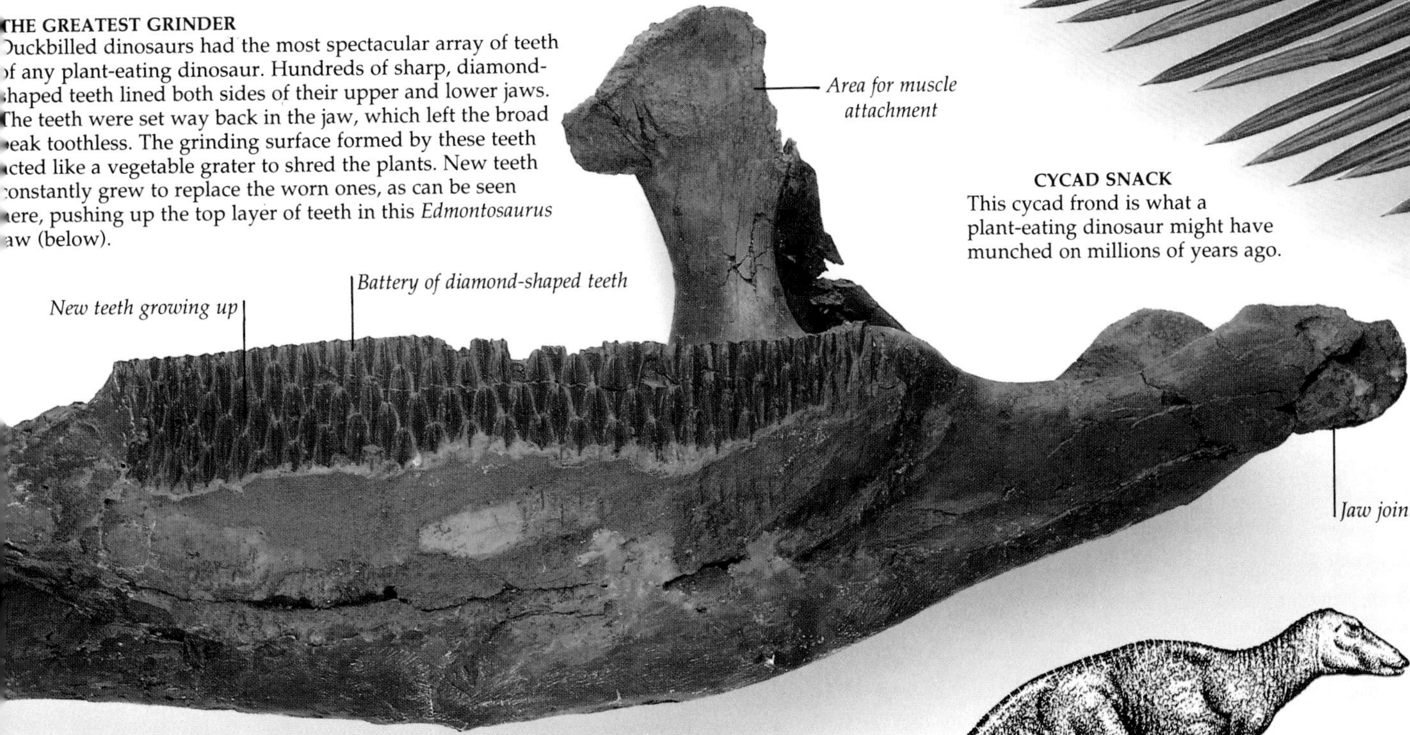

Area for muscle attachment

CYCAD SNACK

This cycad frond is what a plant-eating dinosaur might have munched on millions of years ago.

New teeth growing up

Battery of diamond-shaped teeth

Jaw joint

Sharp edge of tooth for nipping

Edmontosaurus jaw

Area worn down by eating plants

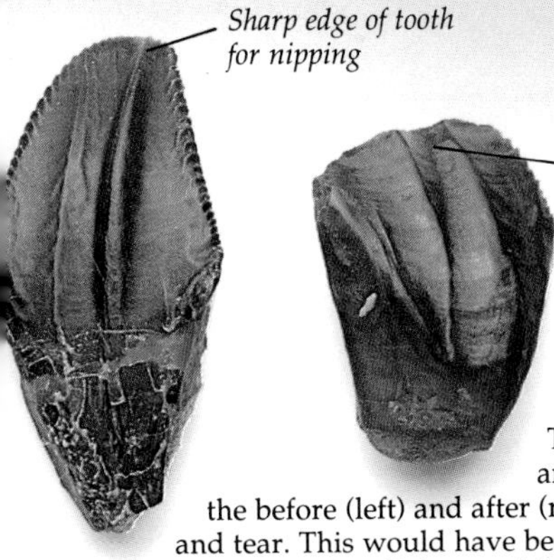

WEAR AND TEAR

Two lower teeth of an *Iguanodon* show the before (left) and after (right) stages of wear and tear. This would have been caused by the tough plant materials cellulose and lignin. Added to this was the unavoidable grit and dust that the animal would have eaten along with the plant.

BELLOWING BEAST

An *Edmontosaurus*, which owned the jaw above, looked like this. It had about 1,000 strong teeth in its cheek region. It may have blown up the loose skin on its flat face to make a loud bellowing call. Duckbilled dinosaurs could also store extra food in their cheeks, like hamsters do.

Edmontosaurus

FOOD FOR THOUGHT

Some of the plants that the dinosaurs used to eat still grow today. These include cycads, horsetails, ferns, and pine trees (pp. 10-11).

Fern leaf

Sauropod peglike tooth

Ankylosaur tooth

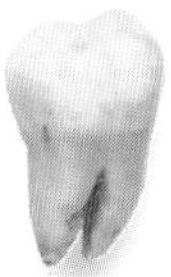

Human molar

DENTAL SELECTION

Sauropods' teeth were either spoon-shaped, for nipping, or peglike, for raking in leaves. The ankylosaurs, or armored dinosaurs (p. 33), had small teeth which were only good for eating soft plants. No dinosaur had flat teeth like human molars, which we use to crush and grind our food.

Sauropod spoonlike tooth

Root

Horsetails

Pine needles

27

Peculiar heads

SOME DINOSAURS HAD most oddly shaped heads, sprouting weird and wonderful projections of bone including lumps, bumps, crests, spikes, and helmets. And just as bizarre shapes or brightly colored patches on reptiles, birds, and even mammals today attract attention, so did the odd shapes of some dinosaurs' heads. They were eye-catching, and could have been used to attract a mate, scare off an enemy, or simply indicate how a dinosaur was feeling – happy or angry! They were often used in attack or defense - a bony head could act like a natural safety helmet, or a formidable head-butting device. The most spectacular heads belonged to a group of dinosaurs called the hadrosaurs, or duckbills, so called because of their broad, toothless beaks.

CREST FALLEN
Different hadrosaurs had different head shapes, but their bodies were all quite similar. Some had heads that were completely unadorned with odd-looking projections. This drawing from 1897 shows one of the most common "crestless" types, *Edmontosaurus*. It used its broad, duck-like beak to scoop up leaves.

HEAD-CASES
The first two heads in this selection are duckbills: *Parasaurolophus*, with its distinctive long horn, and *Corythosaurus*, with its "dinner plate" shaped crest. The broad, thick head on the right belongs to *Pachycephalosaurus*, one of the "boneheaded" dinosaurs.

Toothless beak

Teeth start here

Parasaurolophus skull

28

Long crest was hollow inside

Dome of solid bone

GIVING A HOOT
The long hollow crest on the skull of *Parasaurolophus* has puzzled experts for years. At first it was thought to be a snorkel or a reserve air tank used when the animal was feeding under water. Or perhaps it was an extension of the nostrils, improving the creature's sense of smell. Now we know that the hollow tube was probably a "resonator" through which the dinosaur could bellow or hoot. Females of this species had smaller, less spectacular crests.

Bony spike

THE HEADBANGER
The head of *Pachycephalosaurus* (meaning "thick headed reptile") was 2 ft 7 in (80 cm) long, and its dome was made of solid bone. It used this dome to head-butt enemies, just as sheep and goats use their horns.

Pachycephalosaurus skull

REARING TO GO
Pachycephalosaurus may well have reared up and bellowed loudly, as in the picture, before charging an enemy.

Sharp, pointed beak

Psittacosaurus skull

DUCKBILL DINNER
Because hadrosaurs had toothless beaks, they were often pictured wading in swamps and feeding on soft water plants. But in reality they were mainly land feeders, and could tackle tough vegetation from trees, grinding it up with their powerful jaws (p. 26).

Parasaurolophus feeding

PARROT HEAD
This oddly shaped skull belonged to a *Psitt* or "parrot lizard." This dinosaur did not have many teeth, but it could slice through tough leaves and woody stems with its long, sharp beak.

BIRD BEAK
Psittacosaurus had a sharp beak like a parrot, but there the similarity ended!

Three-horned face

TRICERATOPS, WHICH MEANS "three-horned face," belonged to a group of dinosaurs known as ceratopsians, or horned dinosaurs. Each ceratopsian had a large bony frill pointing backward from the skull and masking the neck, horns on the nose or over the eyes, and a narrow, hooked beak. Most were four-legged and stocky, like the rhinoceroses of today, and all were plant eaters. Many fossils of ceratopsians found in the same area suggest that they roamed in herds, and faced threatening meat eaters as a pack. As the ceratopsians evolved, their headgear gradually became more spectacular. *Triceratops*, the "king" of the ceratopsians, lived at the end of the age of the dinosaurs, and had the most impressive array of horns and frills of all the ceratopsians: its head took up nearly one-third of its length. With head lowered and the horns pointing forward, all backed up by its enormous bulk, *Triceratops* must have been a tough challenge to predators such as *Tyrannosaurus rex* (p. 24).

Brow horn

LIKE A RHINO
This model reconstruction of *Triceratops*, based on the study of complete skeletons of the animal, is probably very close to life. Here, the resemblance to modern rhinoceroses is very striking.

Nose horn

Nostril

Wavy edge of frill

Parrot-like beak

Triceratops skull - front view

SKULL STORY
By far its most prominent feature, *Triceratops'* heavy skull can tell us a lot about its way of life. Its jaw was built to tackle very tough and fibrous plants. It snipped them off with its narrow, hooked beak and then sliced them up with its sharp, scissor-like teeth. The jaws were powered by huge muscles that extended up into the frill. The frill probably acted as an anchor for the jaw muscles, and also protected the neck. *Triceratops* used its sharp horns mainly for defense against tyrannosaurs, but it also used them in one-to-one combat. The male *Triceratops* would lock horns with a member of its own kind and head-wrestle, much as deer, antelope, and sheep do today.

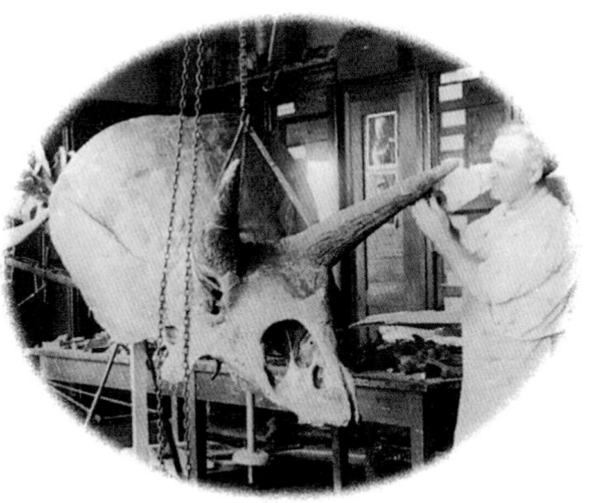

Eye socket

A MAMMOTH TASK
Shown here in the process of reconstruction
is the three-horned skull of
Triceratops.

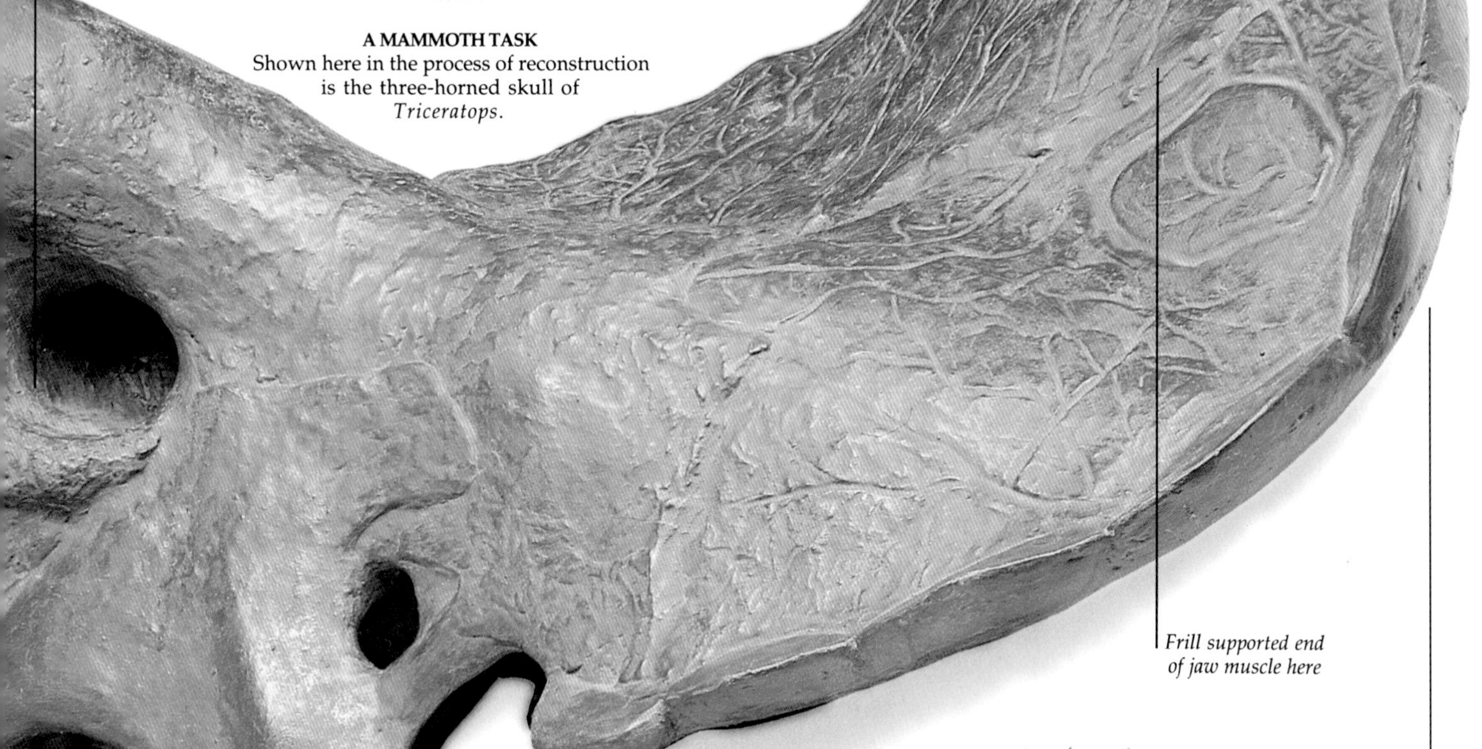

*Frill supported end
of jaw muscle here*

Triceratops
skull - side view

*Jaw muscle was
attached here*

Regal
horned lizard

PRESENT-DAY FRILL
Some living lizards, like this
regal horned lizard, have horns
and frills too. Lizards use their
frills to intimidate enemies,
expanding them to make
themselves look larger than
they really are.

SPIKY STYRACOSAURUS
Roughly half the length of
Triceratops but no less impressive
was *Styracosaurus*. It, too, had
an enlarged nose horn, and its
ill had extra-long spikes, as
ell as several smaller ones.
tyracosaurus would have looked
ery imposing if it lowered its head in display.

A tough skin

Well protected by its bony armor, the armadillo that lives today is like the ankylosaurs, or armored dinosaurs (right). They, too, stayed low to the ground while predators were threatening. Few attackers would have been able to get a grip on their tough bodies.

WHAT WAS dinosaur skin like? Fossilized skin impressions can tell us that it was scaly, like reptile skin, and in some cases armor-plated for extra protection. Dinosaur skin was perfectly suited to life on land. Just like reptile skin, it was waterproof, tough, and horny. Waterproof skin prevents an animal from drying out quickly in air, sun, or wind - animals like frogs have to stay in moist conditions because their skin is thin and not waterproof. Tough, scaly skin protects an animal while it moves around on land, dragging its body over or between rough stones, or falling over. Dinosaur skin impressions, like the ones shown here, are usually small because after death, animal skin rots away too quickly to be fossilized. However, in a few rare cases, an almost entire body impression has been preserved. The dinosaurs that left these impressions probably died in a dry area so that their skin dried out before they were buried by windblown sand. The sand then turned into sandstone over the years, and was so tightly packed against the skin that when the skin disappeared, its exact shape and pattern remained in the stone. No one knows for sure what color dinosaur skin was, or whether it had stripes or spots - dinosaurs are most often shown in muddy shades of green and brown.

COLOR COORDINATED
Dinosaurs may well have had brightly colored skin like this agamid lizard. Skin color can be useful as camouflage or as a warning signal. This lizard probably uses his bright-green skin to mark out a territory or to attract a mate.

SOLITARY NODULE
Bony nodules like this one were mixed in with the overlapping plates on *Polacanthus* skin. These nodules "floated" in the skin beneath the scales, as in living reptiles.

Polacanthus skin impression

A KNOBBY COAT
This knobby skin impression came from an armored dinosaur called *Polacanthus*. Short-legged and squat, it was about 13 ft (4 m) long and had sharp spines running along its back. These, combined with its overlapping bony plates, would have discouraged hungry meat eaters from attacking.

Raised nodules for protection

LIKE A CROCODILE?
Crocodiles are reptiles and have the same type of skin as the dinosaurs - ideally adapted to conditions on dry land. The knobby skin on this "smiling" crocodile is like the *Polacanthus* impression (left).

Central ridge
of nodule

The ankylosaurs had bones
which were fused together
to form a bony armor.
These squat and very
heavy creatures were
the armored tanks
of the dinosaur
world. They looked
much like giant
reptilian armadillos.
They had small jaws
and weak teeth, and
ate plants. They pro-
tected themselves from
large carnivores mainly
by crouching and clinging
to the ground, relying
completely on their tough
skin for defense.

THE COMPLETE BEAST
This is what *Edmontonia*, one of the largest
ankylosaurs, probably looked like when it
was alive. Its armour included spikes that
guarded its shoulders and flanks from attack,
and rows of bony plates.

Smaller scales
for flexibility

ANKYLOSAUR NODULE
Many ankylosaur nodules looked like
this one. The flattened base was
attached to the creature's back, and
the broad central ridge provided
protection. In life, it was covered
by a horny scale (like a fingernail).
In the picture it is possible to
make out the pitted areas
where this was attached.

Sauropod
skin
impression

Bigger scales
where skin
did not have
to bend

UNARMORED AND SCALY
This skin impression, smooth
compared to the ankylosaurs',
came from a sauropod dinosaur,
probably one like *Diplodocus* (pp.
14-21). The skin was scaly, not bony
like the ankylosaur's, and would
have given little protection against
attack. The scales, although
packed tightly together, had
flexible edges where they touched,
which acted like hinges to allow easy
movement. You can see from this
impression that the scales varied in
size, the smaller ones occurring
where the skin
had to bend a lot.

Plated dinosaurs

ONE OF THE MOST unusual groups of dinosaurs were the stegosaurs, named after the North American dinosaur *Stegosaurus*. Easily recognized by the double row of plates running down their backs, stegosaurs also had sharp spikes on the ends of their tails, used for lashing out in defense. Despite their fearsome appearance, these dinosaurs were all plant-eaters. They usually walked on all fours, browsing on low vegetation – a way of feeding that suited their low-slung heads perfectly. Their small, weak teeth could only handle soft plants. The word "stegosaur" actually means "roof lizard," because it was once thought that the plates lay flat on the dinosaur's back, like tiles on a roof. Although this arrangement would have provided slightly better protection against attack from carnosaurs, it is more likely that the plates stood upright in two rows along the stegosaur's back. Some people think that the plates were fixed to the skeleton, but they were actually embedded in the dinosaur's thick skin.

THE PLATE DEBATE
Scientists have long argued about how *Stegosaurus'* plates were arranged. Here they are alternated, but they are often shown in paired rows. The plates were made of bone with honeycomb-like spaces running through – not much use as defensive armor-plating.

A WEIRD STEGOSAUR
This etching shows an early attempt to reconstruct a plated dinosaur – with hedgehog-like spines instead of bony plates! However, there is evidence from hip bone fossils that one stegosaur at least, *Stegosaurus*, could have reared up on its hind legs like this.

Vertebral spine

Cone-shaped plate

Chevron bone

A STING IN THE TAIL
The large, cone-shaped plates on the back of *Tuojiangosaurus* give way to two pairs of sharply pointed spikes, which were used as lethal weapons. Stegosaurs could swing their muscular tails from side to side with great force.

Broad, flat feet

Sharp defensive spike

WARMING UP

Dimetrodon was an early reptile that lived before the dinosaurs. It used the large sail on its back to absorb the heat of the sun on cool days and warm its body. Some plated dinosaurs did the same.

Stegosaurus plate

Some stegosaurs made use of solar power

CLOSE-UP PLATE

Shown at half life-size, this is one of the smaller plates from the neck region of *Stegosaurus*. These large, flat bones acted like the sail of *Dimetrodon* (above left) to warm or cool the animal. The plates were richly supplied with blood, and *Stegosaurus* would have used this blood like water in a central-heating system. Standing in the breeze would have cooled the blood, and basking in the sun would have raised blood temperature, thereby warming the dinosaur.

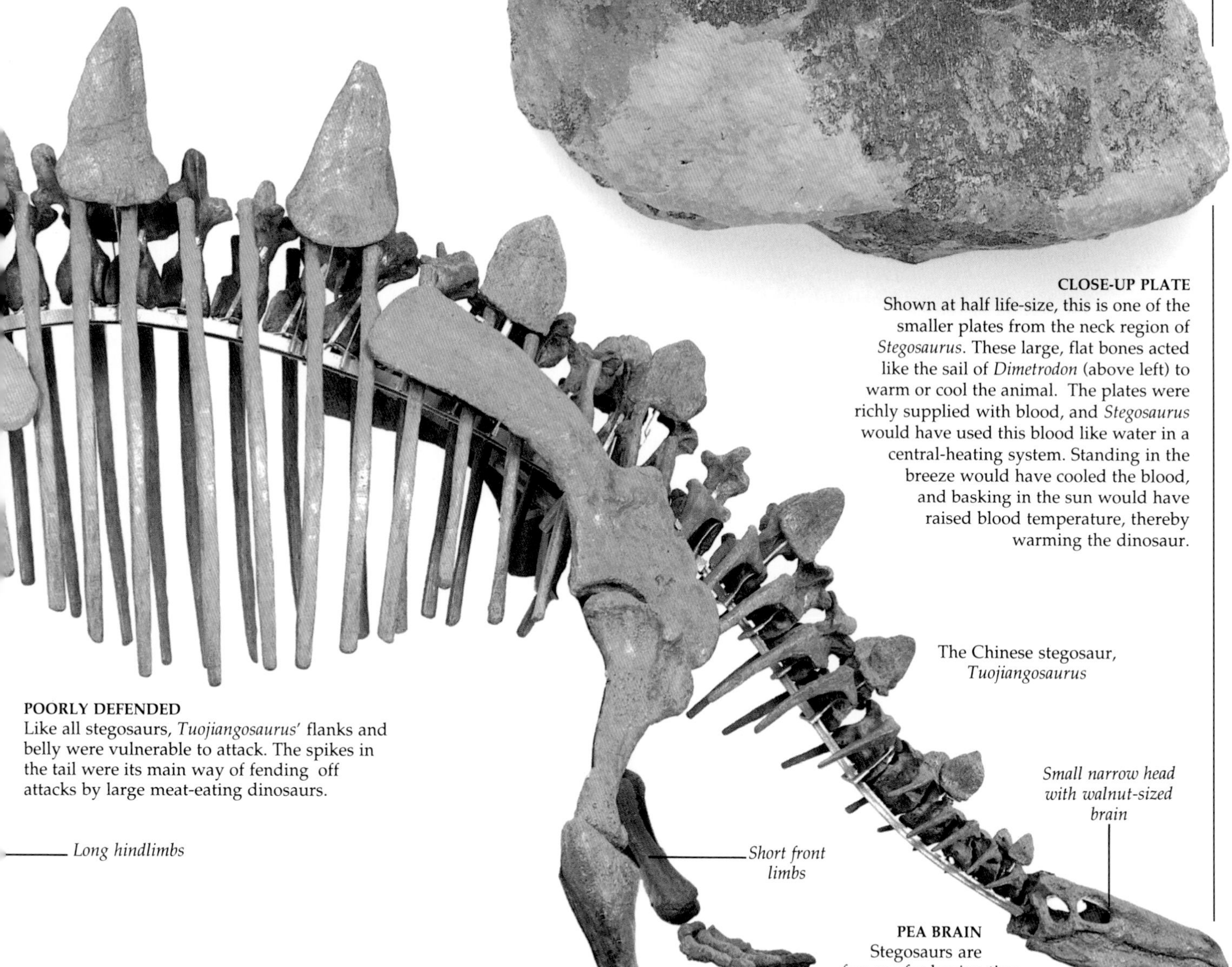

The Chinese stegosaur, *Tuojiangosaurus*

POORLY DEFENDED

Like all stegosaurs, *Tuojiangosaurus'* flanks and belly were vulnerable to attack. The spikes in the tail were its main way of fending off attacks by large meat-eating dinosaurs.

Long hindlimbs

Short front limbs

Small narrow head with walnut-sized brain

PEA BRAIN

Stegosaurs are famous for having tiny brains in proportion to their size. *Stegosaurus* had a brain the size of a walnut. This has given some people the idea that dinosaurs were stupid or slow. But stegosaurs' brains were obviously big enough for their needs, since this creature managed to survive for over 10 million years.

Fast movers

NOT ALL DINOSAURS WERE HUGE and lumbering. Some were built for speed, either to run from attackers, or to chase prey. Unlike fast-running living animals like horses, which are all four-footed, fast-moving dinosaurs ran on their hind legs alone. As a result, all the fast movers looked similar. They all tended to have long back legs, in order to take long strides. Slender legs and narrow feet can be moved quickly and so allowed the dinosaurs to run more efficiently. The rest of the body was usually light and fairly short, balanced by a slender tail. The arms were lightly built, with small-clawed hands, and the neck was long, with a small head on top. Some of the nimble dinosaurs could reach speeds of 35 mph (56 kph) - almost as fast as a racehorse. They could take advantage of their speed in two ways: either to pursue a victim, or to beat a hasty retreat from an attacker. Herbivorous and carnivorous fast-moving dinosaurs were in a kind of "race": plant eaters became faster and faster because only the fastest could avoid being caught by ever-speedier meat eaters.

OSTRICH LOOKALIKE
Struthiomimus, or "ostrich mimic," looked remarkably like an ostrich, and probably ran in a very similar way. Scientists even think it probably had feathers. The main difference is *Struthiomimus'* long bony tail, and its clawed hands in place of wings.

TINY AND TOOTHY
This fast-moving dinosaur, *Heterodontosaurus*, was only about 3 ft (1 m) long. It had three different types of teeth, but was still an herbivore.

Long neck was stretched forward as Gallimimus ran

Gallimimus in motion

Stiffened tail for balancing

A POOR GRIP
Gallimimus, a close relative of *Struthiomimus*, was remarkably birdlike with its toothless beak. Its hands were no adapted for grasping things.

SPRINTING DINOSAURS
Small, agile plant-eating dinosaurs like *Hypsilophodon* (below) were among the fastest runners. By measuring their legs and comparing their shape to those of modern animals, experts have estimated that they reached speeds of 30 mph (45 kph).

Narrow feet for speed

Femur (thigh bone)

Knee joint

The legs of
Hypsilophodon

Strong ankle joints

Slender feet
and toes

Ostrich

NIMBLE HUNTER
At less than 3 ft (1 m) long,
Compsognathus is one of the
smallest known dinosaurs. A meat
eater, it used its agility and speed
to pursue lizards, frogs, and a
variety of other small creatures.

LEGS FOR SPEED
A look at a pair of *Hypsilophodon*
legs shows us special features of
fast-moving dinosaurs. The main
leg bones are slender, yet strong,
and show signs of special bony
attachment areas for powerful
leg muscles. The joints are well
formed, and the feet narrow.
It was once thought that
Hypsilophodon lived in trees,
because of its grasping toes
and balancing tail (p. 62).

SPEEDY BIRD
Apart from their long tails, arms, and bare
skin, many of the small, speedy dinosaurs
were just like ostriches. Ostriches cannot
fly, but they can run as fast as
Hypsilophodon did.

Hypsilophodon in
motion

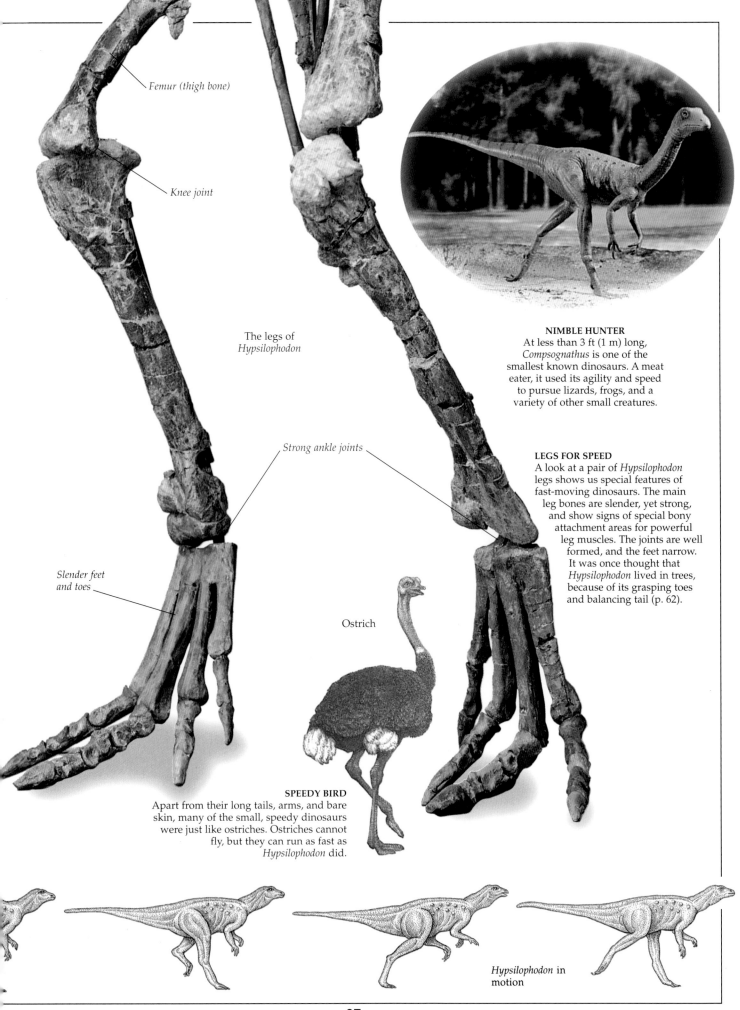

Two feet or four?

WHY DID SOME DINOSAURS WALK on four legs, while others walked on two? The answer is simple: dinosaurs walked in the way that suited their lifestyle best. Most carnivores, for instance, walked on their hind legs, because they needed to use their hands to catch and hold on to their prey. Other dinosaurs usually walked on all four legs, mainly because their enormous size and weight needed support from four sturdy "posts" underneath. However, fossil finds suggest that even a large, heavy herbivore such as *Diplodocus* (p. 14) was able to rear up on its hind legs – for short periods, at least. Some dinosaurs – for example, hadrosaurs – had the option of walking either on two or four legs, depending on what they were doing at the time. Mostly, it suited them to move around slowly on all fours, so that they could browse on low-growing vegetation. When they were alarmed, however, they could rear up and charge off on hind legs alone. These dinosaurs needed special "hands" that allowed for weight support, as well as grasping.

A sauropod mother rears to defend its young

"DON'T COME ANY CLOSER!"
This museum model shows a mother *Barosaurus* rearing up on its two hind legs. It is defending its young against an attack by an *Allosaurus*. However, scientists are still debating whether a huge sauropod would – or could – have behaved like this.

Hooflike claw

Scelidosaurus foot

TOE END
This hadrosaur toe bone from the "hand" is typically flat and hooflike.

Hadrosaur toe

Triceratops toe

FOUR-LEGGED TOE
Triceratops always walked on four legs, so this *Triceratops* toe bone could come from either the front or the back foot. The toe bone is broader and more hooflike than that of the hadrosaur (above), which did not use its front feet so much.

Anklebones

SOMETHING AFOOT?
This is the complete hind foot of an early plant-eating dinosaur called *Scelidosaurus*. It was heavily armored with bony, jaw-breaking studs which ran the length of its body. *Scelidosaurus* always walked on four legs. Its hind foot was strong and broad and had four powerful toes to support the heavy body. The small first toe would have barely reached the ground.

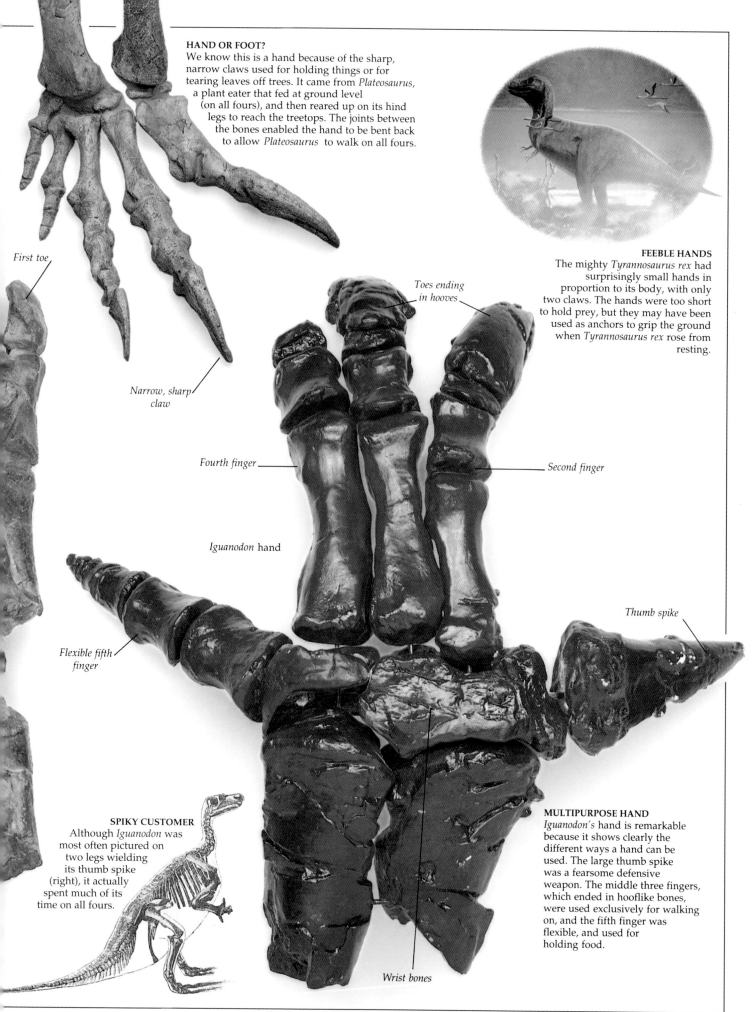

HAND OR FOOT?
We know this is a hand because of the sharp, narrow claws used for holding things or for tearing leaves off trees. It came from *Plateosaurus*, a plant eater that fed at ground level (on all fours), and then reared up on its hind legs to reach the treetops. The joints between the bones enabled the hand to be bent back to allow *Plateosaurus* to walk on all fours.

First toe

Narrow, sharp claw

Toes ending in hooves

FEEBLE HANDS
The mighty *Tyrannosaurus rex* had surprisingly small hands in proportion to its body, with only two claws. The hands were too short to hold prey, but they may have been used as anchors to grip the ground when *Tyrannosaurus rex* rose from resting.

Fourth finger

Second finger

Iguanodon hand

Thumb spike

Flexible fifth finger

SPIKY CUSTOMER
Although *Iguanodon* was most often pictured on two legs wielding its thumb spike (right), it actually spent much of its time on all fours.

MULTIPURPOSE HAND
Iguanodon's hand is remarkable because it shows clearly the different ways a hand can be used. The large thumb spike was a fearsome defensive weapon. The middle three fingers, which ended in hooflike bones, were used exclusively for walking on, and the fifth finger was flexible, and used for holding food.

Wrist bones

Ancient footprints

As WELL AS LEAVING their fossilized bones as evidence, dinosaurs also made their mark on the Earth in the form of footprints. Tracks have been found where dinosaurs walked in soft, swampy land – for example, along riverbanks – in search of food and water. Later on, the prints would have dried and hardened in the sun. Eventually, through rain or flooding, water would have brought more sand or mud, which buried the prints until they gradually fossilized. Called trace fossils, because they are not actually a part of an animal, these footprints can tell us much about how dinosaurs moved. A lot of the same types of prints found together, for instance, with smaller ones in the middle, suggests that some dinosaurs moved in herds, with the young ones protected in the center.

RUNNING ALL OVER THE WORLD
Dinosaur trackways have been found all over the world. These tracks found in Queensland, Australia, came from small meat eaters, running together as a pack. Experts can judge the speed at which they were moving by measuring the distance between the prints.

Toe bone

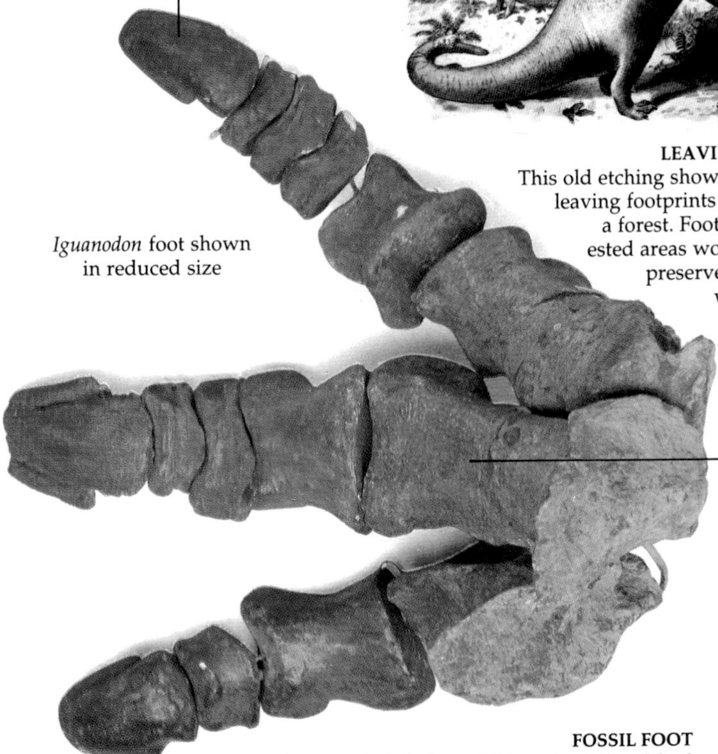

Iguanodon foot shown in reduced size

LEAVING EVIDENCE?
This old etching shows an *Iguanodon* leaving footprints while feeding in a forest. Footprints left in forested areas would not have been preserved, however - they would have had to be made in more swampy land.

Upper foot bone

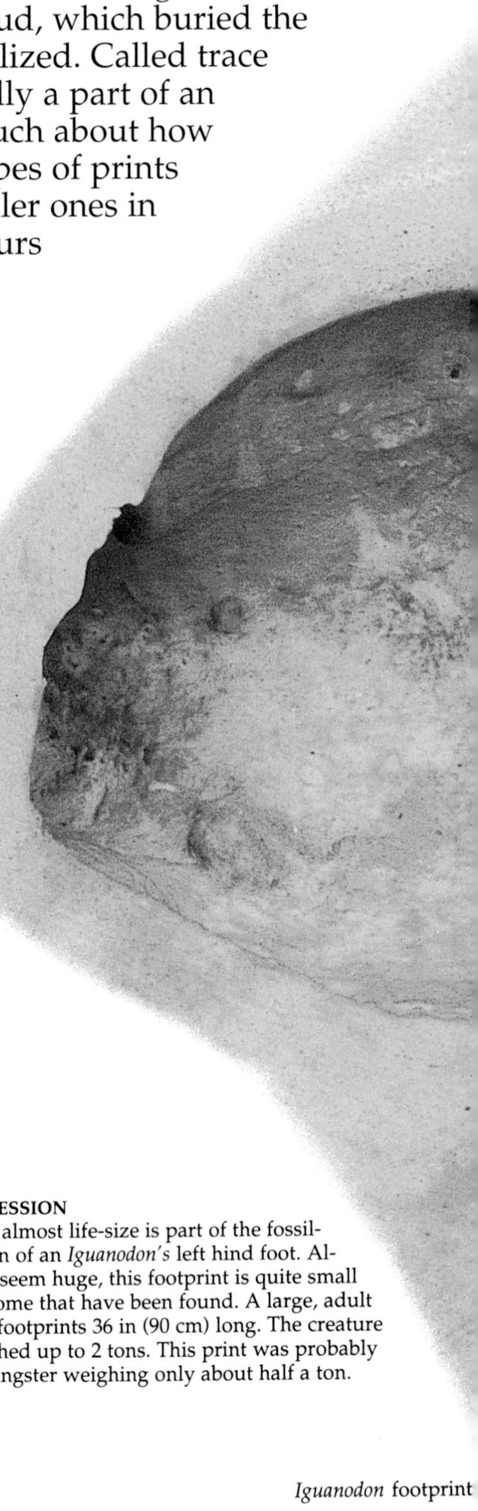

A GOOD IMPRESSION
Shown here in almost life-size is part of the fossilized impression of an *Iguanodon's* left hind foot. Although it may seem huge, this footprint is quite small compared to some that have been found. A large, adult *Iguanodon* left footprints 36 in (90 cm) long. The creature probably weighed up to 2 tons. This print was probably made by a youngster weighing only about half a ton.

FOSSIL FOOT
The three-toed right foot of *Iguanodon* (above) had to be very strong to support the great weight of the animal. *Iguanodon* probably walked on its toes, like cats and dogs do today. The foot leaves a cloverleaf-shaped footprint, many of which have been found in southern England. The heavier the dinosaur, the better the footprint (right).

Iguanodon footprint

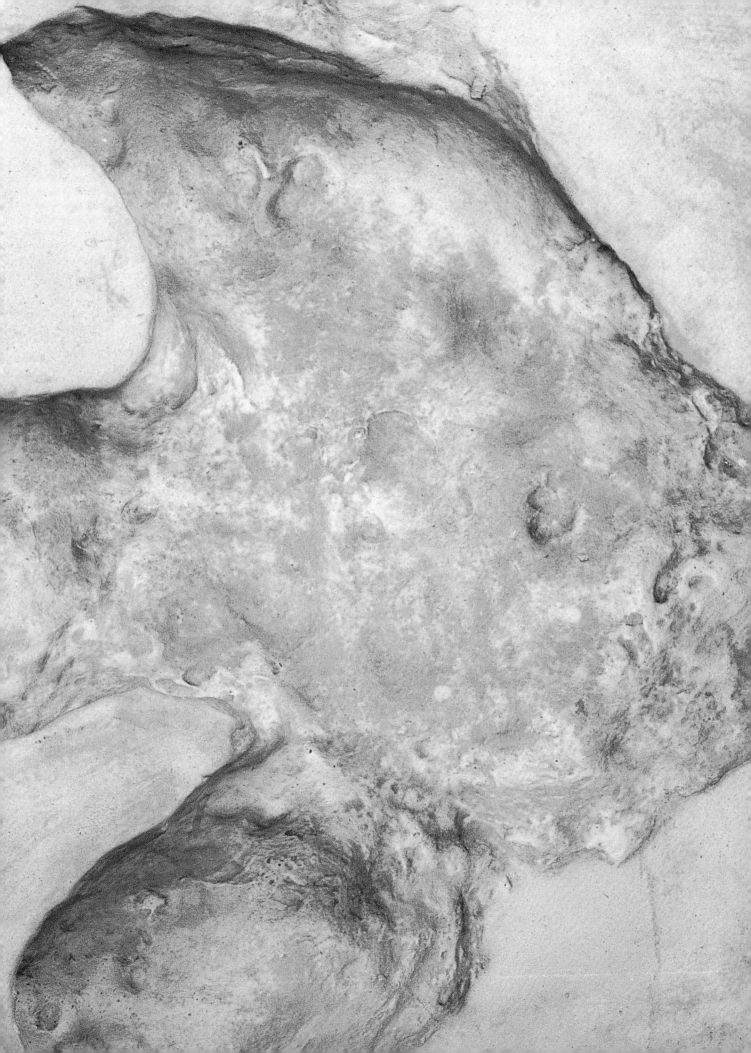

Claws and their uses

CLAW BONES ALL HAVE stories to tell about the lifestyle of their owners. Dinosaurs that hunted and killed other animals tended to have very narrow, sharp, curved claws, like the talons on the foot of an eagle. They used their claws like daggers to gain a secure hold and to keep their unfortunate victim from escaping. The claws also helped to injure or even kill the prey. Perhaps the most terrifying clawed predator of the dinosaur age was *Deinonychus*, or "terrible claw." It had a huge sickle-like claw on its second toe, and long arms with three-clawed hands. It would leap on its victim and slash with its claws, using its long tail to keep its balance. Plant-eating and omnivorous dinosaurs, by contrast, did not have such sharp, talon-like claws. Their claws tended to be broader and more flattened, as they were not needed to kill. They were also stronger and more rugged because they were often put to many uses, such as walking, scraping, and digging for food. Sometimes these hooflike claws were used in self-defense, as crude weapons to slash out at attacking meat eaters.

THUMB CLAW
This smallish claw came from the thumb of *Massospondylus*. The slight swelling at the base was where a strong muscle was attached.

Tubercle (swelling) for strong muscle attachment

"LEAPING LIZARDS"
Caught in action, with their teeth bared, these sparring meat eaters show how they best used their claws - for vicious attack!

CREEPY CLAWS
This feathered dinosaur is *Velociraptor*, or "quick robber." Its jaws were lined with razor-sharp teeth, but its most formidable weapons were four sets of deadly, hooked claws. Using its hand to hold on to its prey, *Velociraptor* would have been agile enough to raise a clawed foot and deliver a killer kick, slashing through its victim's flesh.

Flattened claw

NOT FOR ATTACK
This claw belongs to *Ornithomimus*. Although this dinosaur was a meat-eater, its claws were quite flattened, and would not have been much use for defence or attack.

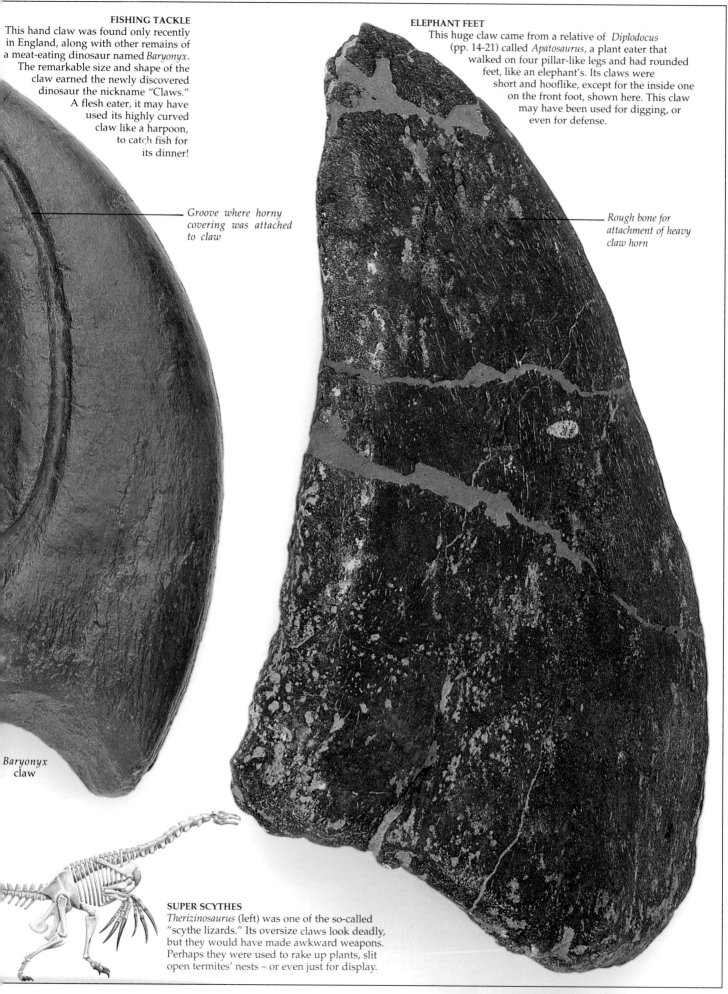

FISHING TACKLE
This hand claw was found only recently in England, along with other remains of a meat-eating dinosaur named *Baryonyx*. The remarkable size and shape of the claw earned the newly discovered dinosaur the nickname "Claws." A flesh eater, it may have used its highly curved claw like a harpoon, to catch fish for its dinner!

Groove where horny covering was attached to claw

Baryonyx claw

ELEPHANT FEET
This huge claw came from a relative of *Diplodocus* (pp. 14-21) called *Apatosaurus*, a plant eater that walked on four pillar-like legs and had rounded feet, like an elephant's. Its claws were short and hooflike, except for the inside one on the front foot, shown here. This claw may have been used for digging, or even for defense.

Rough bone for attachment of heavy claw horn

SUPER SCYTHES
Therizinosaurus (left) was one of the so-called "scythe lizards." Its oversize claws look deadly, but they would have made awkward weapons. Perhaps they were used to rake up plants, slit open termites' nests – or even just for display.

Eggs and nests

A baby *Maiasaura* (p. 46) emerges from its egg

DINOSAURS, LIKE REPTILES and birds today, laid hard-shelled eggs. We know this because many fossilized dinosaur eggs have been found, some even containing small skeletons. Sometimes the eggs have been found in nests, with remains of the parent dinosaurs nearby. Nests found complete with fossilized young tell us that baby dinosaurs, like baby birds, would instinctively stay in their nest, no matter what happened to their mother. Several nests found close together suggest that some dinosaurs nested in colonies. It is perhaps surprising that dinosaur eggs were never huge. If they were in proportion to the size of some adult dinosaurs, the shells would have been far too thick to hatch, and would not have allowed enough oxygen to reach the creatures growing inside.

Cracks which occurred during fossilization

Oviraptor egg

Unidentified dinosaur egg

Quail egg

DINOSAUR AND BIRD
The hatchling that would have emerged from the dinosaur egg (right) would have had lots of growing to do before it was an adult – far more than a chick from a modern bird's egg, such a the quail egg (above).

Textured dinosaur eggshell

GROUND NESTER
This model shows an *Oviraptor* mother brooding its clutch of eggs. Its nest is scraped into a mound, a design that would have stopped the eggs from rolling away and also given some shelter. Like many ground-nesting birds today, *Oviraptor* may have used her body heat to incubate the eggs until they hatched.

A HARD SHELL
This elongated egg was part of the first evidence that dinosaurs laid eggs. They laid their eggs on land, just like lizards do today. The amphibians, from which they evolved, had to lay their eggs in water, where they hatched into tadpoles. Reptiles, however, can lay their eggs on land because the eggs have tough shells with a private "pond" inside for the young to develop safely. Laying eggs like this was probably one of the reasons why the dinosaurs survived on Earth for so long

HE EGG THIEF?

the 1920s, this fossilized nest and
any more like it were discovered in
e Gobi Desert of Mongolia and
hina. For a long time, scientists
lieved the nests belonged to the
orned, plant-eating dinosaur
rotoceratops. When remains of an
viraptor were found on the fossil site,
was thought to have been there as a
avenger, stealing the eggs – the name
viraptor means "egg thief." Gradually,
owever, more and more *Oviraptor*
mains were found. In the 1990s
cientists finally realized that the
ests and eggs belonged to *Oviraptor*,
ot *Protoceratops*.

*Jest in which eggs
ere buried has turned
nto sandstone through
ossilization process*

Birth and growth

BECAUSE MOST OF the dinosaurs were so big, it is hard to imagine them going through baby and juvenile stages in their lives. But recent discoveries have enabled us to piece together a little of their early lives. We know that dinosaur mothers laid their eggs in hollowed-out nests in the ground (pp. 44-45). In some cases, tiny skeletons of hatchlings have been found inside the eggs. Colonies of duckbill dinosaur nests have been found containing skeletons of hatchlings. Their teeth are worn, indicating that the mother dinosaur must have brought food back to the nest. Baby dinosaurs probably grew fast. Sauropods, which moved in herds (p. 12), probably kept their youngsters in the middle as they traveled, protected by the adults on the outside. Some dinosaurs, like the ceratopsians, changed their bodily proportions as they grew up.

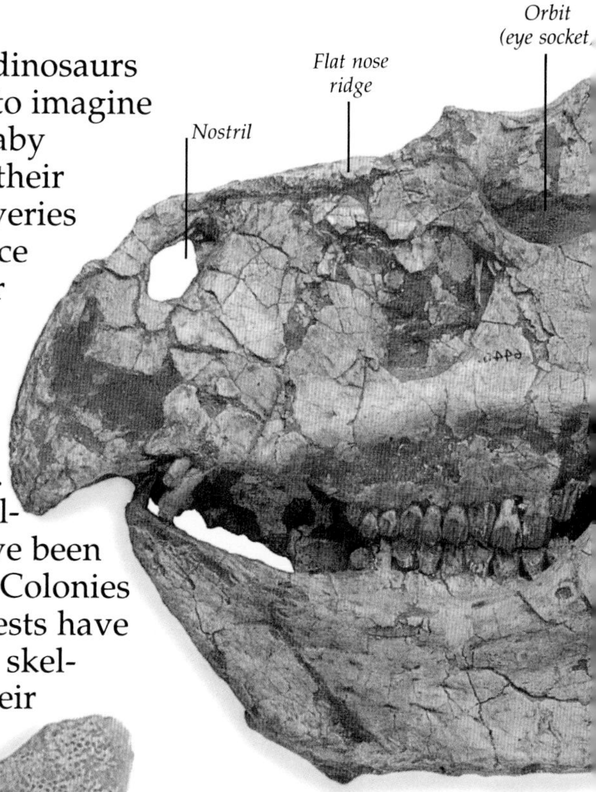

THE NURSERY
This old illustration was drawn when the Gobi Desert eggs were thought to be *Protoceratops'*. It shows how people imagined a dinosaur nursery. There are baby *Protoceratops* at various stages – some hatching, some taking their first steps, some struggling to get out of the sand.

Orbit (eye socket

Flat nose ridge

Nostril

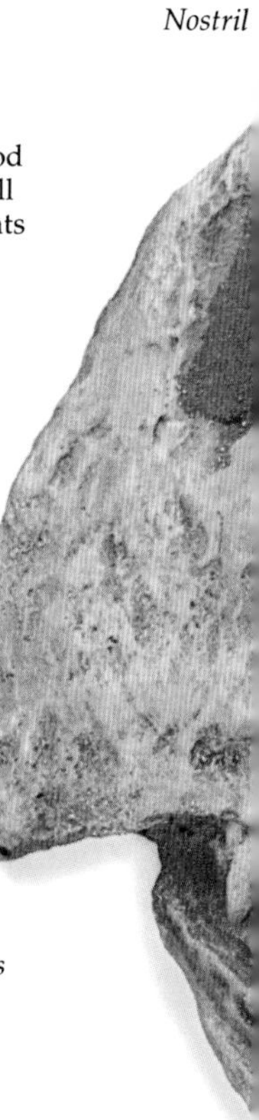

Nostril

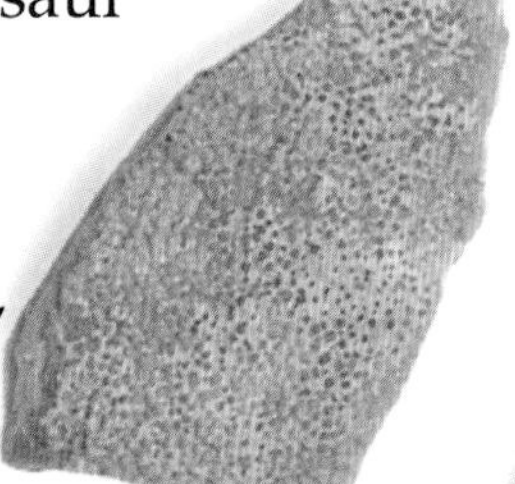

Sauropod eggshell fragments

GIANT SHELLS
These fragments come from large round eggs that were laid by huge sauropod dinosaurs like *Diplodocus* (p. 14).

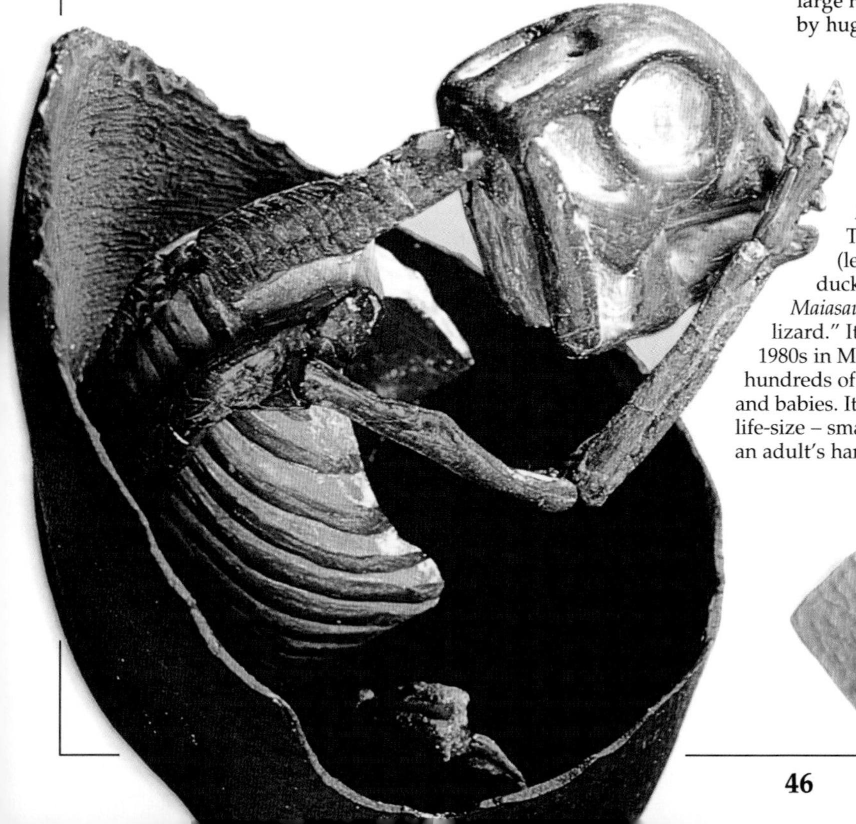

A BEAST EMERGES
This fossilized eggshell (left) contains a hatching duckbill dinosaur called *Maiasaura*, or "good mother lizard." It was found in the 1980s in Montana, along with hundreds of other dinosaur eggs and babies. It is shown here at life-size – small enough to fit in an adult's hand.

Protoceratops eggshell fragments

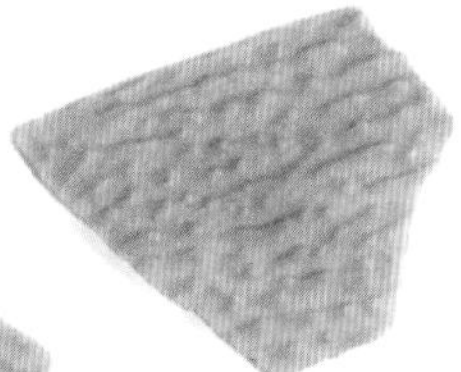

COARSE SHELLS
The coarse, bumpy surface of these *Protoceratops* shell fragments is typical of many dinosaur eggs.

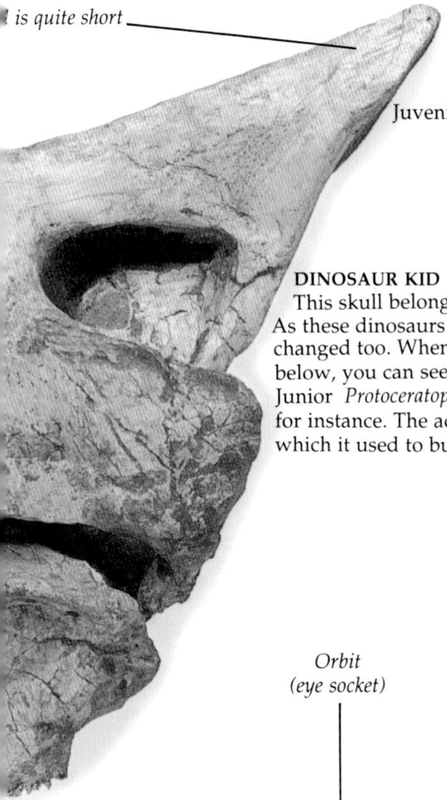

is quite short

Juvenile *Protoceratops* skull

DINOSAUR KID
This skull belonged to a juvenile *Protoceratops.* As these dinosaurs grew, the shape of their skulls changed too. When compared to the adult skull below, you can see just how the proportions altered. Junior *Protoceratops* had a much lower nose ridge, for instance. The adult developed a higher ridge which it used to butt opponents.

Area for attachment of jaw muscles
Big frill for display
Orbit (eye socket)
High nose ridge
Jaw joint
Lower jaw

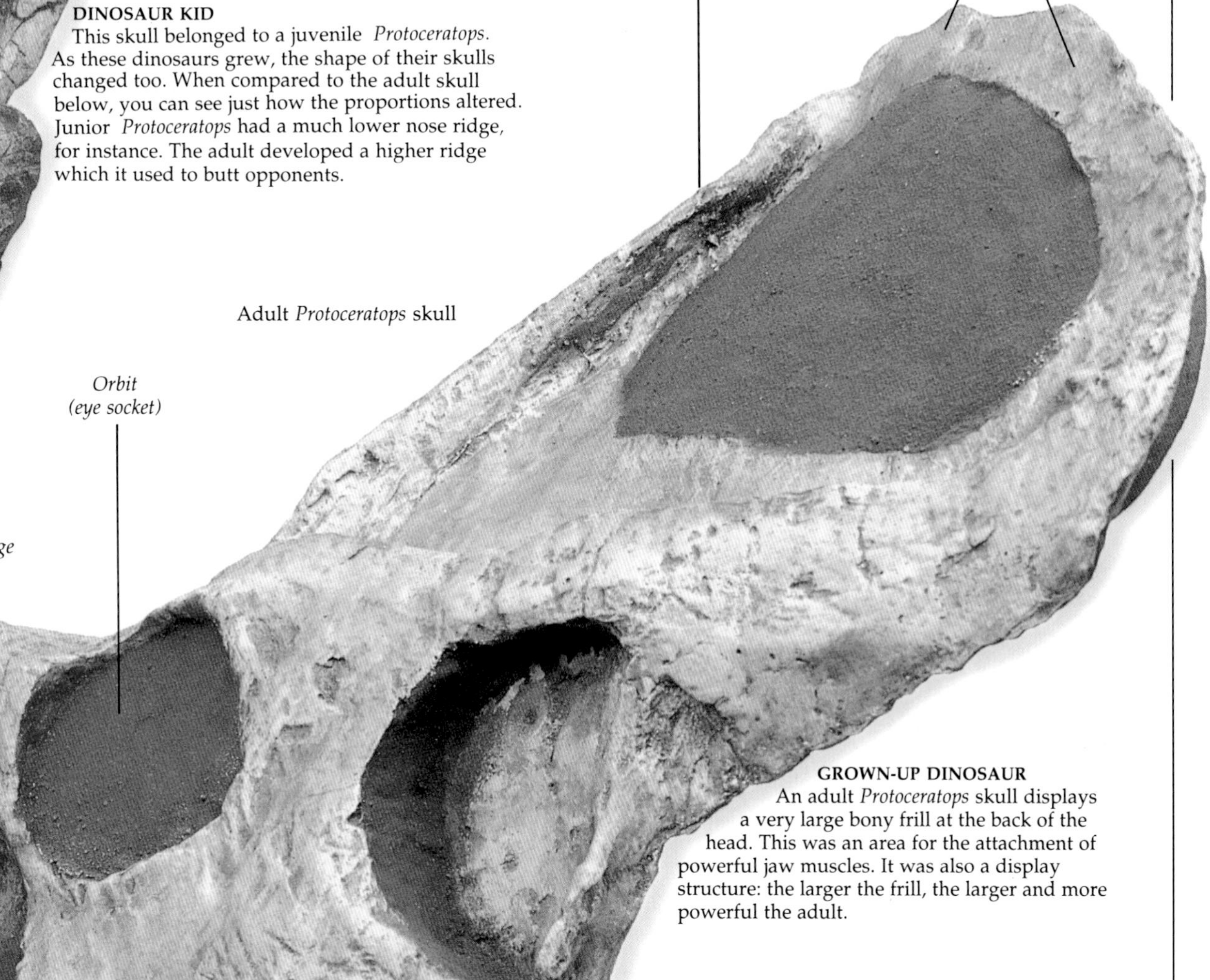

Adult *Protoceratops* skull

GROWN-UP DINOSAUR
An adult *Protoceratops* skull displays a very large bony frill at the back of the head. This was an area for the attachment of powerful jaw muscles. It was also a display structure: the larger the frill, the larger and more powerful the adult.

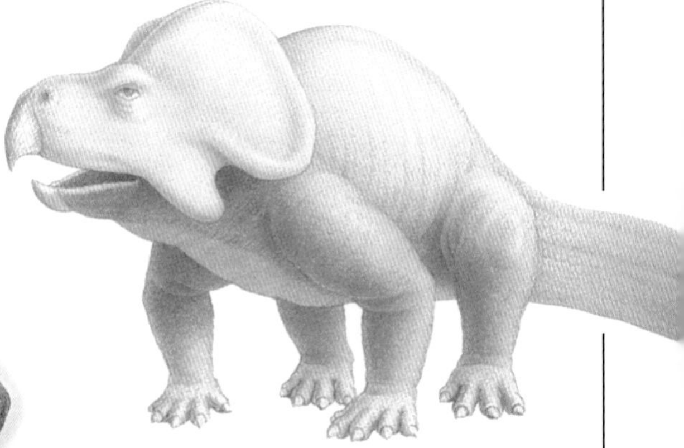

FIRST HORNED FACE
Protoceratops, or "first horned face," was one of the first ceratopians (p. 30). Small and squat, *Protoceratops* was no longer than 6 ft (2 m), and about the height of a large dog.

Death of the dinosaurs

DINOSAURS DISAPPEARED from the Earth quite suddenly, and why this happened is still a mystery. Around 70 million years ago, the dinosaurs ruled the Earth. Yet about five million years later, they had all died out, perhaps only in a matter of months. Scientists have offered various theories to explain their sudden extinction, but many ignore one vital point: dinosaurs were only one of a whole range of creatures that died out at the same time, including all the swimming and flying reptiles. So any theory to explain dinosaur extinction must explain the disappearance of these groups as well. The theories are numerous: some people think that small mammals ate all the dinosaur eggs. This is very unlikely - for how would it account for the extinction of other species that disappeared at the same time? Others believe that a plague of caterpillars ate all the dinosaurs' plant food, and they starved to death.

POISONOUS BITE
It has been suggested that dinosaurs died out because they ate new kinds of poisonous plants, such as deadly nightshade, that started growing on Earth.

Stony meteor fragment

Fossilized ammonite

ROCKS FROM SPACE
A likely reason for the sudden extinction is that a massive meteorite from space collided with the Earth. This would have been catastrophic, causing a huge steam and dust cloud which darkened the Earth for a long time, killing off the plants and the animals that fed on them.

Iron meteorite fragment

A MASS EXTINCTION
Many other creatures died out at the time of the dinosaur extinction. Whatever happened seems to have affected some creatures but left others unscathed. Ammonites (above left), a type of shellfish, became extinct, as did the mosasaurs, plesiosaurs, and ichthyosaurs, groups of meat-eating marine reptiles (above right). Sea crocodiles died out but the river crocodiles survived. The flying reptiles, pterosaurs, disappeared, but birds were unaffected.

Iguanodon ischium (hipbone)

Shaft of ischium bent forward after repair

Section of
hadrosaur backbone

*Vertebral
spine*

**THE BEGINNING
OF THE END**
A *Tyrannosaurus rex*
is shown fleeing in
terror as a meteor hits
the Earth. The impact
would have had an effect
kind of like that of a massive
nuclear war. Dense black clouds of dust and
soot would have cut out the sun for months.

A GROWTH
Dinosaurs could contract cancer. This section of backbone
belonged to a hadrosaur, and shows a swollen area
which was a cancerous tumor in the bone.

*Point of
fracture*

*Thickening of
bone around break*

*Vertebral
body*

*Swollen area of
tumor growth*

BROKEN BONE
During their reign, dinosaurs were not immune to diseases
and accidents. The *Iguanodon* hipbone above shows a fracture
that healed itself during the creature's lifetime.

Dinosaur or bird?

ARE BIRDS THE DESCENDANTS of the dinosaurs? The debate first began with the discovery of a fossil bird, *Archaeopteryx*. It lived 150 million years ago, alongside the dinosaurs. It had feathers, like all birds, but also reptilian features, such as teeth. Could this be the missing link between dinosaurs and birds? *Archaeopteryx* was shown to share over 20 features with meat-eating dinosaurs such as *Coelophysis*, right. One gap in the evidence was the lack of any dinosaur fossils with a wishbone: birds have a well-developed one that helps to keep the wing joint in position. But now we know that several dinosaurs – mainly meat eaters – did have a wishbone. More dramatically, fossil hunters in China have unearthed feather traces belonging to bird-like dinosaurs such as *Caudipteryx* and *Sinornithosaurus*. Some scientists also think theropods in North America, including *Bambiraptor* and *Troodon*, were feathered, but others remain skeptical about the dinosaur–bird link.

BIRDS OF A FEATHER
Archaeopteryx, seen here preening on a ginkgo branch (pp. 10-11), had several distinctly un-bird-like features. It had a long tail with bones down the middle, claws on its wings, and teeth. Its wings were designed for flight, but it is unlikely that *Archaeopteryx* could have flown as well as modern birds.

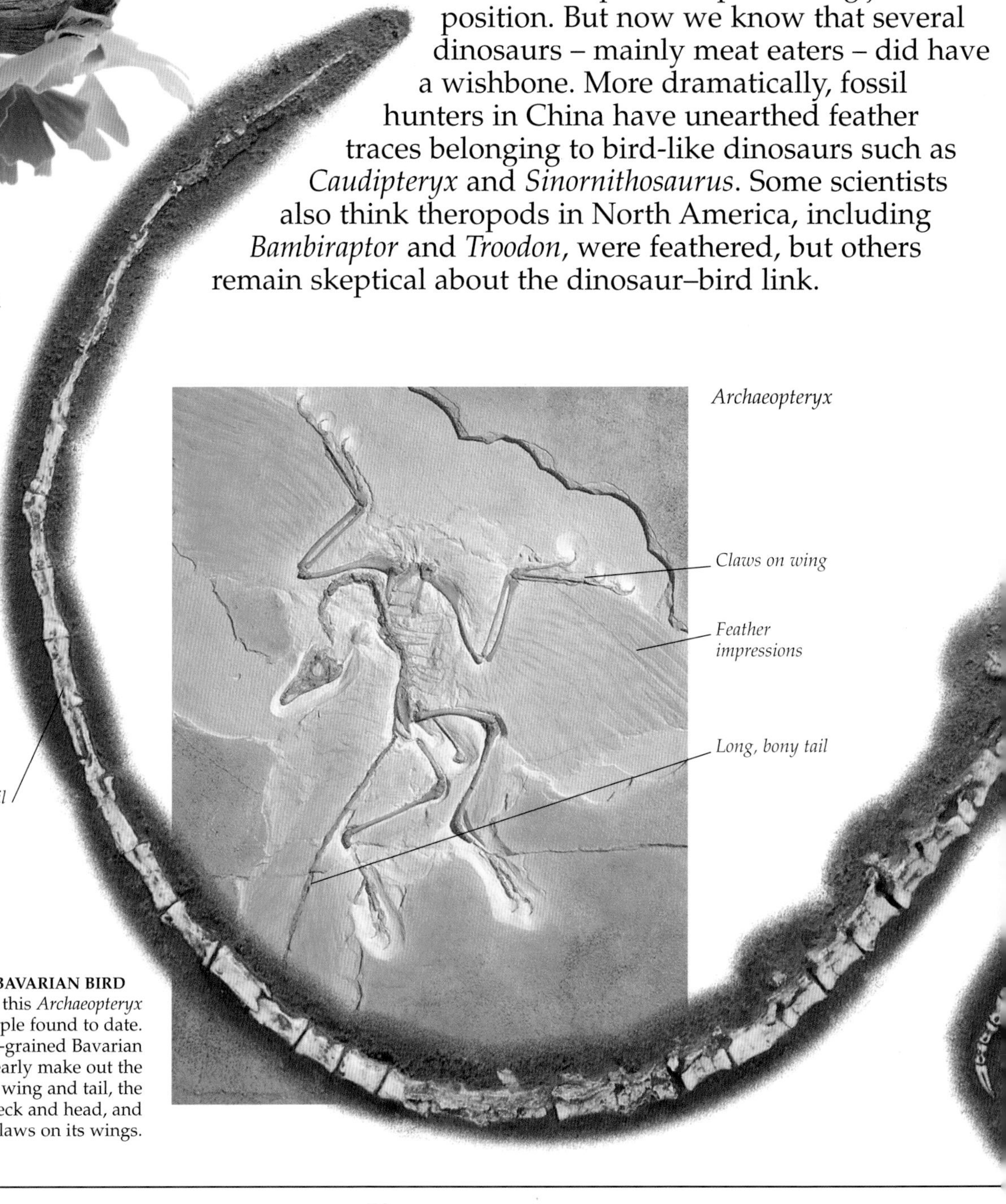

Long tail

BAVARIAN BIRD
Discovered in Germany, this *Archaeopteryx* fossil is the best example found to date. It is preserved in fine-grained Bavarian limestone. You can clearly make out the feathers of the wing and tail, the twisted neck and head, and even the claws on its wings.

Archaeopteryx

Claws on wing

Feather impressions

Long, bony tail

Bambiraptor

A wrist joint like a bird's would have enabled Bambiraptor *to fold its hands as a bird folds its wings*

...SSIL FABLE
...is complete fossil of *Coelophysis*, a small meat-eating
...nosaur, was found at Ghost Ranch in Texas, along with
...any others. It lived right at the beginning of the dinosaur
...e. Lightly built and agile, it had three strong, clawed
...gers on each hand – a feature in common with
...chaeopteryx. In its belly you can see
...nes that are actually the remains of
...ne young of the same species.
... *Coelophysis* may have
...en a cannibal.

Sharp, predatory teeth

Hip region

BAMBIRAPTOR IN ACTION
A bird-like dinosaur called *Bambiraptor*
was discovered in Montana in 1994. It
could not fly, but must
have been a fast
runner, able to
hunt frogs and
small mammals.
It was probably
covered with
downy feathers
that kept in its
body heat.

Coelophysis
skeleton

Bambiraptor
skeleton

BAMBI'S BONES
Bambiraptor had a wishbone and some of its bones
had air sacs, just like the bones of a bird. The dinosaur
also had large eye sockets and a bigger brain cavity
for its size than any other dinosaur. However, its deep
snout and large teeth were not at all bird-like.

Remains of young Coelophysis *in belly*

Caudipteryx

AN EXCITING CHINESE FIND
Caudipteryx was a turkey-sized dinosaur discovered
in China. Its teeth and bones, especially its forward-
pointing pubic bone, indicate that *Caudipteryx* was
a dinosaur. However, it had a beak, feathers, and
short tail. No one really knows what color
Caudipteryx's feathers were. It is possible that
they were brightly colored and used for
spectacular mating displays, as well as
keeping the dinosaur warm.

How to find a dinosaur

THE FIND!
Discoveries of fossil dinosaurs are rare, and best tackled by a team of experienced people.

Hᴏᴡ ᴅᴏ sᴄɪᴇɴᴛɪsᴛs go about discovering dinosaur remains? Because the dinosaurs became fossilized in the first place by being buried in sand, or mud, we know that their fossils can only be found in sedimentary rock - rock that has been built up in layers over the years. Sometimes fossils are found by accident for example by builders digging into the ground. Or fossil collectors may set out deliberately to search an area that is thought to be rich in fossils. Sometimes a large and highly organized scientific expedition is undertaken, based on detailed research. Whatever the method of discovery, careful preparation must be done if the find is to be recovered successfully. Records need to be made of the exact position of the find. And the right tools are needed to ensure that the fossils are removed from the site and returned to the laboratory without being damaged.

DUTCH DISCOVERY
The jaws of the mighty sea lizard *Mosasaurus* were discovered deep in a chalk mine near Maastricht in Holland in 1770. This etching shows the team of discoverers working by torchlight.

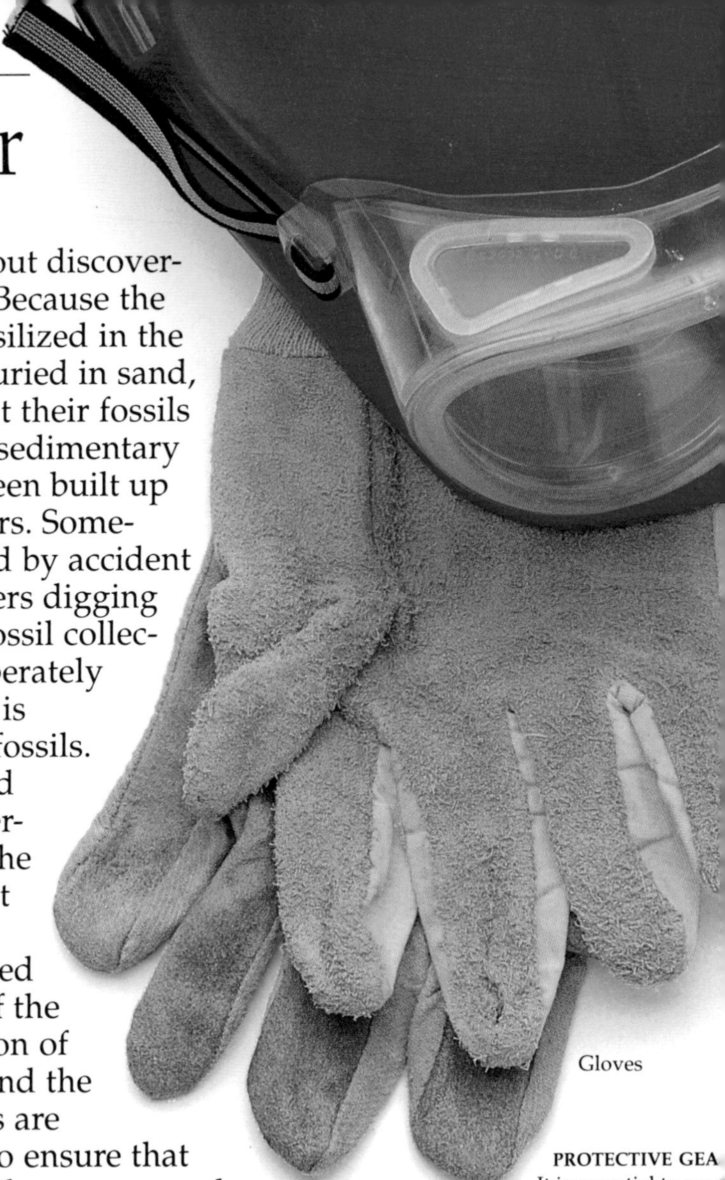

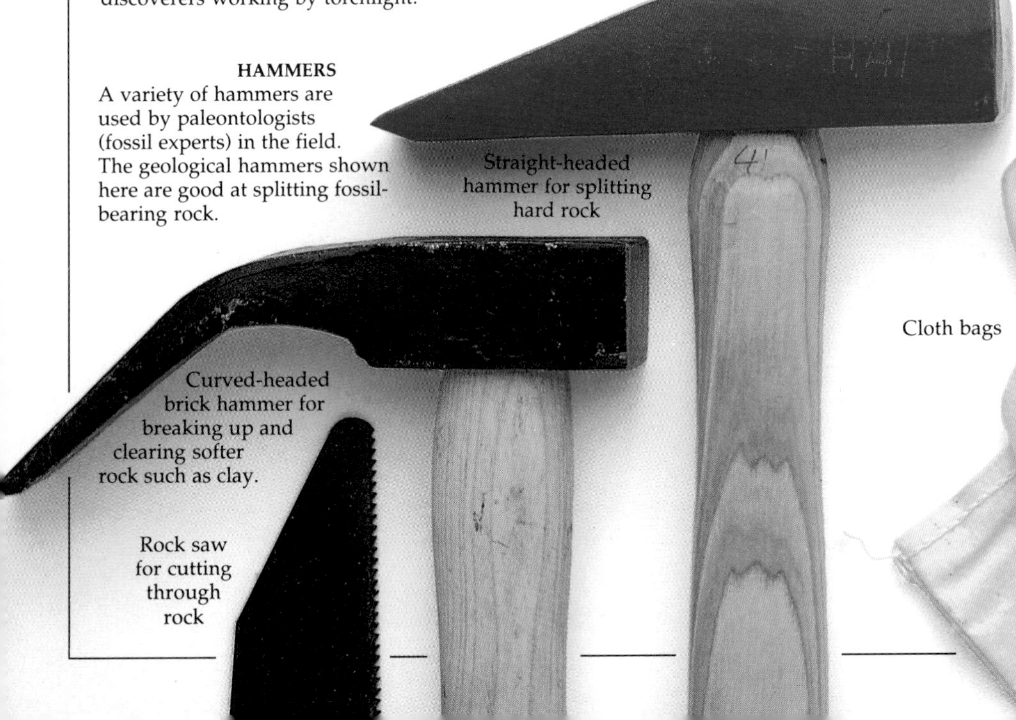

HAMMERS
A variety of hammers are used by paleontologists (fossil experts) in the field. The geological hammers shown here are good at splitting fossil-bearing rock.

Straight-headed hammer for splitting hard rock

Curved-headed brick hammer for breaking up and clearing softer rock such as clay.

Rock saw for cutting through rock

Gloves

PROTECTIVE GEAR
It is essential to wear proper protective clothing while on a fossil dig. Gloves are needed when heavy hammering and chiseling are done, and goggles are used to protect the eyes from splinters of rock. A hard hat is also advisable, especially if work is being done near cliffs.

TAKING NOTES
On a dig, paleontologists always record details of a find and draw a map of the site. Broken fragments and samples of rock are collected in bags and analyzed later back in the laboratory.

Cloth bags

Hard hat and protective goggles

RIBS IN A JACKET
When fossils are partly exposed, they are sometimes encased in plaster jackets to protect them for transportation back to the laboratory. Two ribs of the recently discovered dinosaur *Baryonyx* can be seen in this jacket (pp. 54-55).

Pot of glue

POT AND BRUSHES
Brushes are used to clear away dust while rock is being chipped away around fossils. As a fossil is exposed, it is often painted with a hardener, such as glue, to secure any loose fragments.

Soft paintbrush

Lump hammer

Pointed chisels   Flat chisels

Plastic bags

EXPOSING A FIND
When the rock in which the fossil is embedded is very hard, a heavy hammer and chisels are needed. This lump hammer is used to drive chisels into the rock. It is useful to have a wide variety of chisels for getting into awkward corners.

Clipboard with drawing of the site, and notebook with field notes

Hard paintbrush

Baryonyx ribs encased in plaster jacket

Aluminum foil covers fossil

PROTECTING THE FIND
A paleontologist on a dig carefully covers a fossil with a plaster jacket.

FOAM JACKET
Sometimes fossils are protected by a polyurethane foam jacket. The fossil is first wrapped in foil, then the chemicals to make the foam are poured over it. The foam expands and surrounds the fossil, which can then be moved safely. Because foam gives off toxic gases as it is mixed, it is not recommended for use except by professionals.

Polyurethane foam jacket

RAW MATERIALS
To make a plaster jacket, the plaster is mixed with water to make a paste, then the scrim is dipped into it. The rock and fossil are covered with a layer of wet tissue paper before the scrim and plaster are applied. This keeps the plaster from sticking to the rock and fossil.

Roll of plasterer's scrim (open-weave fabric), and plaster of Paris

How to rebuild a dinosaur

Iguanodon foot bone

Cartilage cap of ankle joint

Ligament scars

AFTER THE HARD work of excavation, the precious fossils are taken back to the laboratory for preparation, study, and display. This whole process is a lengthy one. First, the fossil remains need to be carefully removed from their protective jackets (p. 53). Then, the remaining rock or earth in which the fossil was originally buried has to be cleaned away. Chisels are used on hard pieces of rock, or more delicate power-driven tools (like dentists' drills), for detailed work. Sometimes chemicals are used to dissolve away the surplus rock. The cleaned bones are then carefully studied in order to understand how they fitted together, and therefore how the dinosaur lived. Some tell-tale clues are to be found on the actual surface of bones, because muscles sometimes leave clear marks where they were attached. These marks can be used to reconstruct dinosaur muscles, or flesh.

CLUES FROM THE BONE
This foot bone from Iguanodon provides many clues of muscle attachment during life. At the upper left end its surface is roughened for attachment of cartilage (gristle) of the ankle joint, and along its length are ligament scars for attachment to other bones. The rough area at the bottom of the bone is a cartilage joint surface for the middle toe

Cartilage surface of joint for toe

ON DISPLAY
Museums often display fossil replicas, cast from molds of the real, delicate fossils. This *Barosaurus* reproduction is being erected in the American Museum of Natural History. Not all scientists agree that *Barosaurus* could rear like this.

Making a model

Many museums display cutaway reconstructions of dinosaurs, like the one below. The starting point is a scale drawing that details how the bones and muscles fitted together. Based on this, an armature (framework) is built from wire and wood. A sculptor shapes modeling clay around the armature, adding in details such as bones and skin texture. The clay model is used to create a rubber mold, so that a resin version can be cast. Finally, the cast is handpainted and airbrushed.

Preliminary sketch

Wire and wood armature

Finished clay model

Rubber mold

Painted and finished cast

DIGITAL DINOSAURS
Computers now create superb 3-D reconstructions of dinosaurs and other prehistoric creatures, such as this pareiasaur (right). Digital models can be viewed from all angles and even shown in motion.

Baryonyx neck
vertebra

A LOAD OF OLD BONES
During the 19th century, when dinosaurs had just been
discovered (pp. 8-9), the sculptor Benjamin Waterhouse
Hawkins built models of dinosaurs first in England,
then in the United States. This shows his work-
shop in New York.

*Faint
scratches*

A NECK BONE
This neck bone
belonged to the
newly discovered dinosaur
Baryonyx, seen reconstructed
opposite. The bone has a
complicated shape and
was buried in very hard rock,
so it took a long time to
prepare. The faint scratches
that can be seen are where
rock remains to be cleared.

AN ACID BATH
Sometimes, in laboratories,
vats of acid are used to dissolve away rock from fossils
without damaging them. The
chemicals used in this process
can be very dangerous, so protective clothing must always be worn
when lowering the fossil into the vat.

IN DEATH THROES
Baryonyx is shown here as it looked
after it died. It sank to the bottom
of a lake where it gradually
became fossilized. Such a
realistic model shows how
the skills of the scientist
and model-maker can be
brought together to great
effect. The way that
the dinosaur was lying
was worked out from
the position in which
the bones were found.

Model of *Baryonyx* as it looked after it died

The timescale

IT IS INCREDIBLE TO THINK that animals and plants have lived on Earth for over 700 million years. During this time a bewildering variety has come and gone. The first dinosaurs appeared about 210 million years ago (mya) at the end of what is known as the Triassic period. They roamed the Earth throughout the Jurassic period until 64 million years ago, right at the end of the Cretaceous period. During the millions of years of life on Earth, the world has changed enormously: continents have moved, sea levels and climates have changed, creatures have become extinct. If we look at fossils of creatures that lived before, during, and after the dinosaur age, we can see how some things have changed, and some have remained much the same.

At the time when the dinosaurs appeared, none of the countries of the world existed as we know them - the world consisted of one huge landmass called Pangaea.

TRILOBITE
This creature lived on the seabed and scuttled around on sharp, spiny legs. Although abundant in the early oceans, it was extinct long before the first dinosaurs appeared.

IN THE MISTS OF TIME
This is what the world may have looked like during the dinosaur age. Dinosaurs lived through three periods of time: the Triassic, from 230 to 195 mya, the Jurassic, from 195 to 141 mya, and the Cretaceous, from 141 to 65 mya.

■ **260 mya:**
AMPHIBIAN
Amphibians lived before and during the dinosaur age, and are still with us today. Frogs, for instance, are amphibians. They can breathe and move on land, but have to lay their eggs in water (p. 44).

A BEETLE
Beetles are a group with a very long history, and were probably the prey of early reptiles and amphibians, just as they are today.

Small sharp teeth

■ **260 mya:**
EARLY REPTILE
This is the underside of the skull of an early lizard-like reptile called *Captorhinus*. It may have eaten small insects and snails with its small sharp teeth.

■ **230 mya:**
COELACANTH FISH
The earliest known coelacanth appeared 390 million years ago. These fish were thought to be extinct, but recently many living coelacanths have been discovered.

Spaces for jaw muscle

■ **230 mya:**
PROCOLOPHON
This is the skull of a small early reptile which fed on roots and tubers.

SCORPION STORY
Living scorpions belong to an ancient group which dates back about 400 million years.

■ **230 mya:**
DIICTODON
The owner of this mammal-like reptile skull was squat and pig-shaped. It ate plants and lived during the early Triassic period.

LIVING FOSSIL
This lungfish has fossil relatives which date back 390 million years.

200 mya:
MEGAZOSTRODON:
This furry model is based on a tiny skeleton that was found a few years ago. It was one of the earliest true mammals, and lived alongside the early dinosaurs.

Eye socket

205 mya:
MASSETOGNATHUS
The last mammal-like reptiles that appeared just before the early dinosaurs were large and doglike in appearance. Mammal-like reptiles became extinct when the dinosaurs appeared, but smaller, rodent-like mammals survived.

200 mya:
ICHTHYOSAUR
Ichthyosaurs were swimming reptiles which flourished throughout the dinosaur age. This paddle - once a limb - would have been used by the animal to propel itself along in the water. Ichthyosaurs had long, narrow, pointed snouts.

Long narrow snout

200 mya:
CROCODILE
The shape of a crocodile skull has not changed very much over the years. A long snout lined with teeth is one of the best tools for catching swimming prey. The snout on this crocodile is particularly narrow, which suggests that it must have been very partial to fish.

210 mya:
RIOJASUCHUS
This skull belonged to a creature that lived just before the early dinosaurs, one of the thecodonts or "socket toothed" reptiles. It was built like a long-legged crocodile, and had powerful teeth and jaws.

The story continues. . .

Two *Thecodontosaurus* feeding

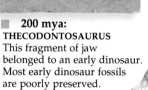

200 mya:
THECODONTOSAURUS
This fragment of jaw belonged to an early dinosaur. Most early dinosaur fossils are poorly preserved.

STAYING POWER
Crocodiles lived before, during, and after the reign of the dinosaurs, and are still around today. Being aggressive river-dwelling predators obviously suits them very well.

EARLY DAYS
Thecodontosaurus could eat both plants and meat (p. 23). One of these two is feeding on cycads; the other is about to pounce on a lizard.

■ **160 mya:**
CROCODILE
Crocodile scutes, or plates, like this square bony one are often found in rocks that also yield dinosaur remains. This suggests that crocodiles may have scavenged dinosaur carcasses.

■ **155 mya:**
PLESIOSAUR
This tooth belonged to a plesiosaur, a fierce marine reptile that lived at the same time as ichthyosaurs (p. 57). They lived during the Jurassic period.

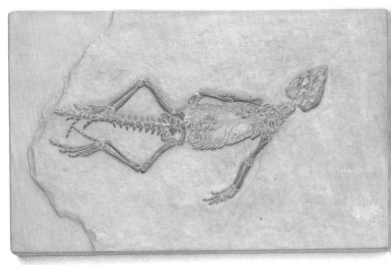

■**147 mya: SPHENODONTID LIZARD**
Lizard-like reptiles such as this specimen have a very long history. They lived throughout the reign of the dinosaurs.

Modern dragonfly

Fossil dragonfly

■ **140 mya:**
DATED DRAGONFLY
Dragonflies can be called "living fossils": they were flying in the skies 320 million years ago, and still exist today.

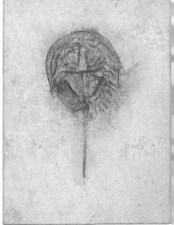

■ **140 mya:**
KING CRAB
King crabs are only remotely related to crabs. They have been around since before the dinosaur age, and still live today.

■ **140 mya:**
GRYODUS
Many types of bony fish like this one lived at the same time as the dinosaurs. Most were fossilized in fine lake sediments, so they are preserved in great detail.

■ **145 mya:**
PTERODACTYLUS
Flying reptiles called pterosaurs flew in the skies while the dinosaurs ruled the land. Some were the size of sparrows; others were as big as small aircraft. The larger ones would have swooped down to catch fish in the waters, while smaller ones, like this *Pterodactylus* (right), would have caught insects in the air.

Gray plover

DAWN OF THE BIRDS
The first birds appeared in the late Jurassic period - about 150 mya. But they did not come into their own and rule the skies until the pterosaurs became extinct (at the same time as the dinosaurs).

The cockroach is one of nature's great survivors. Cockroaches have lived on Earth since long before the dinosaur age, and, judging by their success at living in human environments, they seem set to survive for a long time to come.

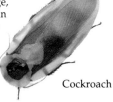

Cockroach

COME FLY. . .
In the Jurassic Period, a sky scene at dawn or dusk would have been crowded with pterosaurs darting through the air catching prey. Their place is taken today by birds that feed on the wing: swifts, housemartins, and swallows.

■ **136 mya:**
DRYOSAURUS
This femur (thigh bone) belonged to a small, fast-moving, plant-eating dinosaur. It used its speed to flee fierce predators.

Dryosaurus femur

Water moccasin snake

SNAKES ON THE SCENE
Slithering snakes arrived on the scene in the late Cretaceous period. They are like modified legless lizards.

■ **120 mya:**
LIZARD'S JAW
This fragment of jaw came from a lizard like the sphenodontid preserved in rock, above left. Fragments like this are found more often than complete specimens.

■ **120 mya:**
CROCODILE
The crocodile that owned this skull (right) lived in the early Cretaceous period.

■ **115 mya:**
IGUANODON
This is a tail bone from *Iguanodon*, a plant-eating dinosaur (pp. 8-9). *Iguanodon* lived only in the Cretaceous period.

■ **120 mya: TEETH**
These fierce-looking stumpy crocodile teeth are preserved from 120 million years ago, but are very like the teeth that belong to living crocodiles today.

The story continues. . .

■ **120 mya:**
SCUTE
This scute, part of a crocodile's bony armor, comes from a crocodile that lived during the Cretaceous period.

■ **110 mya:**
GASTROPOD
Many different snails lived during the dinosaur age.

The end of an era

As THE CRETACEOUS PERIOD drew to a close, the dinosaurs became gradually less numerous, until eventually they disappeared altogether. At the same time changes were also taking place in the Earth's landscape. The continents became separated by wide stretches of sea. Sea levels rose, flooding much of the low-lying land where many types of dinosaur lived. Many groups of sea animals became extinct. Instead of being warm all the time, the climate began to become more variable, or seasonal. The types of plants living at the time also changed: flowering plants became increasingly abundant. As the dinosaurs died out, they made way for a new ruling group on Earth: the mammals.

NOT LONG TO LIVE
The mosasaurs lived only at the end of the Cretaceous period, and became extinct alongside the dinosaurs.

■ 70 mya:
MOSASAUR
This giant marine lizard used its large pointed teeth to crack open shells of animals such as ammonites (p. 48).

Turtle shell

■ 90 mya:
ALBERTOSAURUS
The owner of this toe bone was a large meat-eating dinosaur. Few of these meat eaters survived up to the end of the dinosaur age.

■ 95 mya:
TURTLE
This turtle shell is a relic from the Cretaceous period. Turtles were another group that survived the mass extinction.

Scales

■ 100 mya:
ICHTHYOSAUR
These sharp, pointed teeth, now embedded in rock, belonged to an ichthyosaur (p. 57). Marine reptiles like this all became extinct at the same time as the dinosaurs.

■ 75 mya:
CRAB
Crabs, like their lobster relatives, survived the extinction (p. 58).

Crab

■ 85 mya:
MARSUPIAL
This jaw bone belonged to a pouched mammal (like a kangaroo). Marsupials, now found mainly in Australia, lived alongside the dinosaurs, and were able to evolve rapidly after they disappeared.

■ 90 mya:
BONY FISH
Bony ray-finned fish were another group that suffered very little damage during the "great extinction."

■ 100 mya:
LOBSTER
Some marine groups, like lobsters, were barely affected by the mass extinction at the end of the Cretaceous period. Why some groups became extinct and others didn't is to this day a great mystery.

■ 100 mya:
LEAF
Broad leaves like this one are typical of flowering plants that appeared during the Cretaceous period.

BONY HERRING
The bony fish we are familiar with today are very like those that lived in the late Cretaceous.

Hawksbill turtle

TURTLE TALE
Turtles and tortoises belong to a group of reptiles that have changed very little in appearance since their origins 200 million years ago.

■ **55 mya:**
TURTLE SKULL

■ **25 mya:**
SHARK TOOTH
Sharks have been around for 400 million years and have changed very little.

Cricket

Spider

Hyracotherium (early horse) skull

■ **35 mya:**
INSECTS IN AMBER
This cricket and spider were perfectly preserved millions of years ago, because they became trapped in amber, fossilized resin that drips from pine trees.

■ **50 mya:**
EARLY HORSE
Horses appeared soon after the dinosaurs became extinct, and soon there were many different types of horses grazing on the new plants and grasses that were growing. Early horses had toes, not hooves, on their feet.

■ **1 mya:**
HOMO ERECTUS
Human beings were one of the last species to arrive on the ever-changing scene on Earth. Early species of humans date back a mere one million years (64 million years after the last dinosaur died). In this "short" period of time, people have risen to dominate most of the land and are beginning to have a notice-able effect on the environment.

Human skull

Early rodent skull

■ **35 mya:**
EARLY RODENT
Gnawing animals like rats and mice did not exist until well after the dinosaurs died, and are still thriving today.

■ **40 mya:**
LIZARD
This jaw belonged to a land lizard. Although all the giant marine lizards like mosasaurs became extinct with the dinosaurs, the small land-living ones were unaffected.

A BRACHIOPOD
Brachiopods, or lampshells, one of the oldest animal groups, are little changed from those found in rocks 500 million years old.

THE BUZZING BEGINS
Brightly colored flowers and flower scents seemed to herald the arrival of butterflies and bees. Attracted by the colors and scents of the flowers, butterflies, bees, and other insects carried pollen from one flower to another, just like they do today.

Red rose

FLOWER POWER
The flowering plants that appeared early in the Cretaceous period soon began to dominate the plant world.

Myths and legends

DINOSAUR DRAGON
The winged dragon of mythology looks a lot like some dinosaurs, except for the wings. Some people see dragons and dinosaurs as being one and the same. But the big difference is that dragons never existed!

WHEN DINOSAUR BONES were first discovered, people found it hard to believe that these creatures had actually lived on Earth. They associated the dinosaurs with terrifying monsters. Because so little was known about them, many mistakes were made at the beginning. Dinosaur bones were put together in the wrong way (p. 8), or even mixed up with other creatures' bones. Today, misconceptions about dinosaurs are just as common. Visitors to museums often think that the dinosaurs walked around looking like living skeletons! Politicians and writers sometimes unfairly use dinosaurs to describe something that is old-fashioned, out of date, useless, or inefficient. It is common to think that dinosaurs were big, dull, stupid, and headed for extinction because they were poorly designed to cope with the world in which they lived. In fact, nothing could be further from the truth. Dinosaurs were among the most elegant and sophisticated animals that the Earth has ever seen. They survived for nearly 150 million years - 75 times longer than humans have lived on Earth.

A WATERY END
A common misbelief is that dinosaurs were sea monsters, possibly still lurking in the ocean depths. In fact, no dinosaur was purely sea living. The sea reptiles that shared the dinosaur world were mostly plesiosaurs and ichthyosaurs.

DINOSAURS IN THE TREES
When *Hypsilophodon*, a small, agile, plant-eating dinosaur, was first discovered, it was thought to live in trees. In fact, it was believed to be the dinosaur equivalent of a tree kangaroo that lives in Papua New Guinea. Scientists thought its long tail helped it to balance in the trees, and special sharp toes on its feet helped it to cling to branches. Now this theory has been proved wrong. In fact, *Hypsilophodon* was a ground-dwelling dinosaur that used its stiff tail as a stabilizer while running.

BRONTOSAURUS BLUNDERS
Scientists do the best they can with the evidence available, but early models of *Apatosaurus*, originally called *Brontosaurus*, were based on a mix-up. Its skeleton had been dug up but it lacked a skull, and its bones became muddled up with another sauropod, *Camarasaurus*. Museum reconstructions showed "*Brontosaurus*" with a short, round skull until the 1980s, when its real skull was found, proving to be much like the skull of *Diplodocus* (p. 22).

CHINESE DRAGONS
The mythical dragon is an important symbol in Chinese culture, and it seems likely that it originated from the discovery of dinosaur remains. The Chinese have been collecting dinosaur fossils for over 2,000 years, but referring to them as dragon bones. Even today "dragons' teeth," which are mostly fossil dinosaur teeth, are collected and ground into powders for use as medicines, as they are thought to have healing properties.

Two Hypsilophodon dinosaurs perched in a tree

Special grasping toes

Balancing tail

Grasping hand to hold branch

DINOSAURS AND CAVE DWELLERS
Some films and cartoons have given the impression that dinosaurs shared the Earth with early people. In fact, dinosaurs became extinct 64 million years before the first people ever appeared on the Earth!

Did you know?

AMAZING FACTS

Iguanodon is one of the most common dinosaurs. In one location, between 1878–81, coal miners in Belgium dug up more than 39 *Iguanodon* skeletons.

Baryonyx claw

One of the rarest dinosaurs known is *Baryonyx*. So far, only one specimen has been found. It includes a 6-in (30 cm)-long thumb claw.

Dinosaur fossils have been discovered in rocks from the Triassic Period. One of the earliest dinosaurs may have been *Eoraptor*, which was discovered in Argentina in 1991. Its name means "dawn (or early) plunderer lizard," because this meat-eater lived about 228 million years ago, at the beginning of the dinosaur era.

Remains of dinosaurs have been discovered in Madagascar, Africa, which may be older than *Eoraptor*, at around 234 million years old. However, the remains are in poor condition and scientists are still debating the find.

The earliest-known carnosaur is *Piatnitzkysaurus*, from the Jurassic Period.

Fossilized skin of *Saltasaurus*

The first dinosaur named was the carnosaur *Megalosaurus*, in 1824.

The name ornithomimid means "bird-mimic reptile" because scientists think these dinosaurs were built like flightless, long-legged birds, such as ostriches.

All that scientists knew of *Troodon* for several years was a single tooth—the name "troodontid" means "wounding tooth."

Troodon is the best-known troodontid. It had large eyes and a relatively large brain for its body size, giving it the reputation of being one of the most intelligent dinosaurs and a successful hunter. Scientists base this theory on the similarity of the optic nerve channels and brain cases of fossils with those of modern predatory creatures.

Troodontid fossils are rare, partly because their thin bones were not easily preserved.

Dromaeosaurid means "running lizard." These small, aggressive hunters were probably both swift and lethal, with their blade-like fangs, clawed hands, and huge switchblade claws on their second toes.

Fossils of the small plant-eater *Protoceratops* are so abundant in the Gobi Desert in Mongolia that fossil-hunting palaeontologists there call it the "sheep of the Gobi."

A tangled fossil found in the Gobi Desert in 1971 shows a *Protoceratops* and a *Velociraptor* fighting. The *Velociraptor* had grasped the plant-eater's snout while kicking its throat. The *Protoceratops* had gripped its attacker's arm in its strong beak. The animals may have died from their wounds or been killed by a fall of sand from a nearby dune.

Scientists used to think that the ankylosaurs were the only armored dinosaurs until the discovery of an armored sauropod, *Saltasaurus*. Its armor consisted of large bony plates covered by smaller, bony nodules, and probably covered its back and sides.

Coprolites—preserved dung—contain the remains of what dinosaurs ate, such as bone fragments, fish scales, or the remains of plants. Scientists can study them to find out about dinosaur diets.

A dinosaur egg can only be firmly identified if an embryo is preserved in it. So far, this has only been possible with *Troodon, Hypacrosaurus, Maiasaura, Oviraptor,* and, recently, a titanosaur (see next page).

The first complete titanosaur skeleton was found in Madagascar in July 2001. Titanosaurs grew to around 50 ft (15 m) long, but their bones were relatively light, so few have survived.

Tyrannosaurus had the reputation of being the largest meat-eater for many years, but lost that title in 1993 when an even larger meat-eater (*Giganotosaurus carolinii*) was discovered in southern Argentina.

Giganotosaurus is thought to have been as heavy as 125 people, with a head twice the size of that of *Allosaurus*.

Large eyes absorb more light, improving night vision

Troodon

Dinosaur footprints are far more common than fossil dinosaur bones. They are often given their own scientific names because it is difficult to tell which particular animal made a particular footprint.

Few dinosaur tracks show the marks of a tail, which suggests that dinosaurs walked with their tails held off the ground.

QUESTIONS AND ANSWERS

Q How many types of dinosaur are there?

A So far, about 700 species of dinosaur have been named. However, half of these are based on incomplete skeletons, so some may not be separate species. About 540 dinosaur genera have been named. Of this number, about 300 are considered to be valid genera. Most genera contain only one species, but some have more. Some scientists believe that there may be 800 or so dinosaur genera still to be discovered.

Q How are dinosaurs named?

A Dinosaurs may be named after a feature of ther bodies (such as *Triceratops*, meaning three-horned face), the place where they were found (such as *Argentinosaurus*), or after a person involved in the discovery, such as *Herrerasaurus*

Titanosaur eggs

(Herrera's lizard). An animal name usually consists of the genus and the species name. For example, the biological name for humans is *Homo* (genus) *sapiens* (species).

Q How did dinosaurs communicate?

A Scientists believe that dinosaurs probably communicated through sound and visual displays. The chambered crests on the heads of some dinosaurs, such as *Parasaurolophus*, may have amplified grunts or calls. It is thought that forest-living dinosaurs made high-pitched sounds that carried through the trees. Those that lived on the plains may have made low-pitched sounds that would carry well along the ground. Visual displays could have included posturing, such as pawing the ground or shaking the head.

Psittacosaurus, meaning "parrot lizard"

Q Were dinosaurs warm- or cold-blooded?

A The debate still rages about whether dinosaurs were warm-blooded, like mammals, or cold-blooded, like reptiles. Swift and agile predators, such as *Deinonychus*, would indicate a warm-blooded mode of life. Also, some dinosaurs have now been found with feathers, and only warm-blooded animals would need such insulation. However, some dinosaurs, such as *Stegosaurus*, had plates on their backs, possibly to collect heat from the Sun, which suggests they were cold-blooded. In 2000, research was published on the discovery of the first-ever fossilized dinosaur heart (in 1993). Many scientists dispute the findings. However, the research suggests that the heart was similar to those of birds and different from those of modern-day reptiles, so some dinosaurs at least were probably warm-blooded.

Q What color were the dinosaurs?

A Paleontologists do not know for sure, but they think that most dinosaurs may have been as brightly colored as modern-day reptiles (such as snakes and lizards) and birds. Some may have had patterned skin to help them hide in vegetation. Others may have had bright warning colors to scare off predators or as a kind of display to help them find a mate.

Q Who found thousands of dinosaur eggs?

A In 1997, a group of Argentinian and American scientists discovered thousands of grapefruit-sized rocks littering a dry, barren area in Patagonia, South America. As they neared the site, they realized the "rocks" were fossilized dinosaur eggs. Some of the eggs contained embryos, so the scientists were able to work out that the unborn babies were probably titanosaurs. The mothers would have returned to the same nesting grounds each year.

Record Breakers

BIGGEST DINOSAUR
Seismosaurus ("earth-shaking lizard") probably measured around 110 ft (34 m) and weighed up to 29.5 tons (30 tonnes). Some scientists believe *Argentinosaurus* was ever larger overall, weighing 49 tons (50 tonnes). However, skeletons of both are incomplete.

BIGGEST MEAT-EATER
Theropods *Giganotosaurus* ("huge lizard") and *Carcharodontosaurus* ("shark-toothed lizard") were both nearly 46 ft (14 m) long.

BIGGEST HEAD
Including its head shield, the head of ceratopian *Torosaurus* measured 9 ft (2.8 m) long—longer than a sedan.

LONGEST NECK
The neck of *Mamenchisaurus* measured up to 32 ft (9.8 m) and contained 19 vertebrae, making up almost half of the animal's total body length.

SMALLEST BRAIN
Stegosaurus had the smallest brain of any known dinosaur. It weighed about 2.5 oz (70 g) and was the size of a walnut.

LONGEST DINOSAUR NAME
Micropachycephalosaurus

SHORTEST DINOSAUR NAME
Minmi

Stegosaurus

Classification of dinosaurs

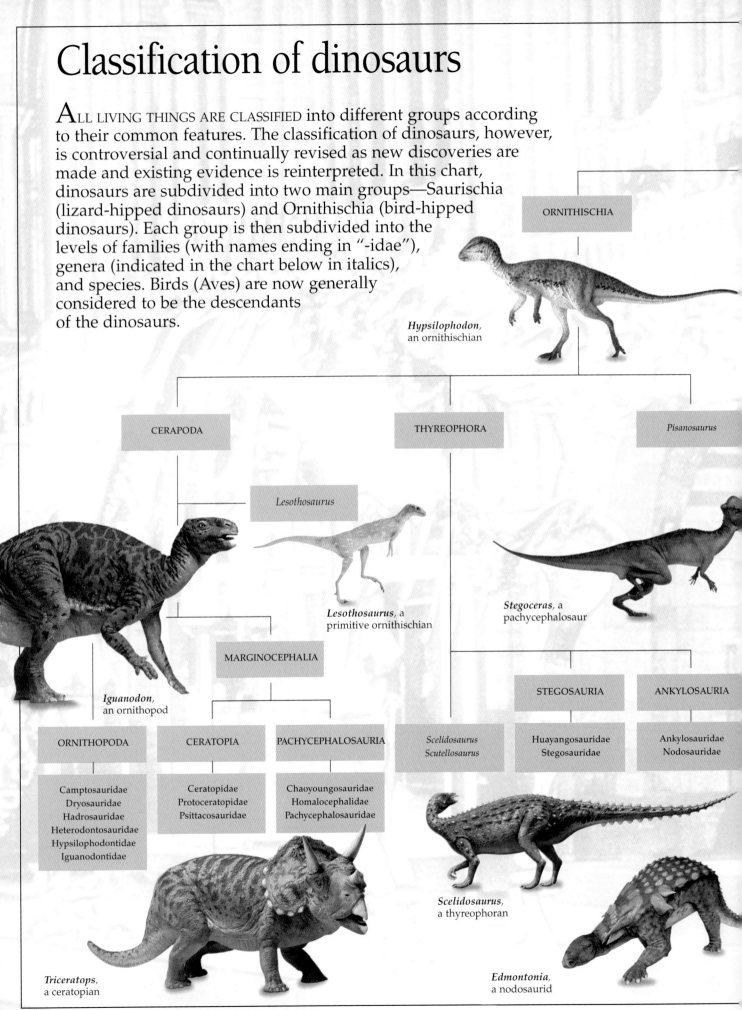

ALL LIVING THINGS ARE CLASSIFIED into different groups according to their common features. The classification of dinosaurs, however, is controversial and continually revised as new discoveries are made and existing evidence is reinterpreted. In this chart, dinosaurs are subdivided into two main groups—Saurischia (lizard-hipped dinosaurs) and Ornithischia (bird-hipped dinosaurs). Each group is then subdivided into the levels of families (with names ending in "-idae"), genera (indicated in the chart below in italics), and species. Birds (Aves) are now generally considered to be the descendants of the dinosaurs.

ORNITHISCHIA

Hypsilophodon, an ornithischian

CERAPODA

THYREOPHORA

Pisanosaurus

Lesothosaurus

Lesothosaurus, a primitive ornithischian

Stegoceras, a pachycephalosaur

Iguanodon, an ornithopod

MARGINOCEPHALIA

STEGOSAURIA

ANKYLOSAURIA

ORNITHOPODA

CERATOPIA

PACHYCEPHALOSAURIA

Scelidosaurus
Scutellosaurus

Huayangosauridae
Stegosauridae

Ankylosauridae
Nodosauridae

Camptosauridae
Dryosauridae
Hadrosauridae
Heterodontosauridae
Hypsilophodontidae
Iguanodontidae

Ceratopidae
Protoceratopidae
Psittacosauridae

Chaoyoungosauridae
Homalocephalidae
Pachycephalosauridae

Scelidosaurus, a thyreophoran

Triceratops, a ceratopian

Edmontonia, a nodosaurid

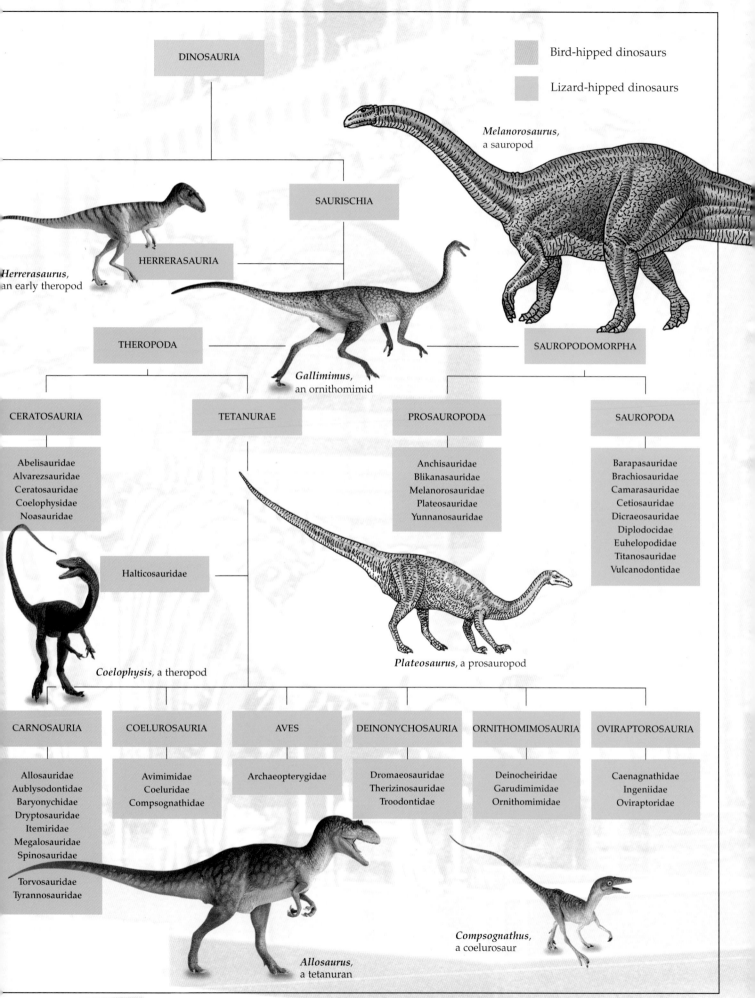

DINOSAURIA

Bird-hipped dinosaurs

Lizard-hipped dinosaurs

Melanorosaurus, a sauropod

SAURISCHIA

Herrerasaurus, an early theropod

HERRERASAURIA

THEROPODA

SAUROPODOMORPHA

Gallimimus, an ornithomimid

CERATOSAURIA

Abelisauridae
Alvarezsauridae
Ceratosauridae
Coelophysidae
Noasauridae

TETANURAE

PROSAUROPODA

Anchisauridae
Blikanasauridae
Melanorosauridae
Plateosauridae
Yunnanosauridae

SAUROPODA

Barapasauridae
Brachiosauridae
Camarasauridae
Cetiosauridae
Dicraeosauridae
Diplodocidae
Euhelopodidae
Titanosauridae
Vulcanodontidae

Halticosauridae

Coelophysis, a theropod

Plateosaurus, a prosauropod

CARNOSAURIA

Allosauridae
Aublysodontidae
Baryonychidae
Dryptosauridae
Itemiridae
Megalosauridae
Spinosauridae

Torvosauridae
Tyrannosauridae

COELUROSAURIA

Avimimidae
Coeluridae
Compsognathidae

AVES

Archaeopterygidae

DEINONYCHOSAURIA

Dromaeosauridae
Therizinosauridae
Troodontidae

ORNITHOMIMOSAURIA

Deinocheiridae
Garudimimidae
Ornithomimidae

OVIRAPTOROSAURIA

Caenagnathidae
Ingeniidae
Oviraptoridae

Compsognathus, a coelurosaur

Allosaurus, a tetanuran

Find out more

MANY PEOPLE ARE FASCINATED by dinosaurs, so even though these amazing creatures died out millions of years ago and no human has even seen one, there are plenty of places to find out more about them. Museums of natural history or specialist dinosaur museums display life-sized reconstructions, often with sound effects or moving parts. You can also take a virtual tour of many museums over the internet if you cannot visit them in person. Television shows, such as Discovery Channel's *Walking with Dinosaurs*, or movies such as *Jurassic Park* also give fascinating and realistic portrayals of the age of the dinosaurs.

GO FOSSIL HUNTING
A great deal of research is made before any organized fossil-hunting expeditions by paleontologists. Even so, some important dinosaur discoveries have been made by amateur fossil-hunters where fossil-bearing rocks have been exposed. Eroding cliffs are the best places to find fossils, especially on seashores. Before starting any such search, collectors must make sure they get permission to visit a site, if necessary. Care must also be taken at coastal sites to stay away from overhangs and watch for the incoming tide.

Realistic dinosaur model from the movie The Lost World, *based on the novel by Sir Arthur Conan Doyle and filmed in New Zealand in 2001*

ON A DINO DIG
It is possible to arrange to go on an actual dinosaur dig or watch scientists at work in the field. For example, at the Dinosaur National Monument Quarry in Utah (right), visitors can see excavation of fossils in progress. The Wyoming Dinosaur Center also offers dig tours where you can join paleotechnicians on an active dinosaur dig. For more information, log on to their website at http://server1.wyodino.org/index.

SEE A MOVIE!
Recent movies and television programs use computer-generated imagery (in which many of the visuals are created and animated by computer software) to portray dinosaurs. *Jurassic Park* was the first movie to employ paleontologists as advisers and to present dinosaurs as realistically as possible. Before then, dinosaurs were brought to life for the screen by such methods as sticking horns on lizards (*Journey to the Center of the Earth*, 1958), or manipulating puppets off-screen (*The Land That Time Forgot*, 1974).

Computer animatronics bring a herd of stampeding dinosaurs to life in the third *Jurassic Park* movie.

Full-sized mechanical model of an allosaur, used for close-up shots in The Lost World *in conjunction with computer-generated images*

BEHIND THE SCENES
Original fossil bones are extremely heavy, so modern reconstructions usually use lightweight casts to make the mounting easier. The original bones are then housed in museum storerooms and used for research purposes. Many museums have laboratories where scientists study dinosaurs and other fossils. Some museums offer visitors the opportunity to watch scientists at work.

THE WYOMING DINOSAUR CENTER AND DIG SITES
Thermopolis, Wyoming
www.wyodino.org
This large museum is host to more than 50 active dig sites. Highlights include:
• 20 full-size mounted skeletons, including 10 dinosaurs
• tours of active dig sites with explanations of how dinosaur bones are found.

NATURAL HISTORY MUSEUM OF LOS ANGELES COUNTY
Los Angeles, California
www.nhm.org
The largest natural and historical museum in the western United States has a large collection of dinosaurs, including:
• "Dueling Dinosaurs"—complete skeletons of a *Tyrannosaurus rex* and *Triceratops* in battle
• a cast of the longest-necked dinosaur ever discovered
• one of the finest *Tyrannosaurus rex* skulls on view anywhere.

AMERICAN MUSEUM OF NATURAL HISTORY
New York, New York
www.amnh.org
Famous for its series of fossil halls, this museum currently has the largest number of dinosaur skeletons on display. Highlights include:
• *Tyrannosaurus, Apatosaurus,* and *Maniraptor* skeletons
• the cast of the only juvenile *Stegoceras* ever found, plus skin impressions of *Edmontosaurus* and *Corythosaurus.*

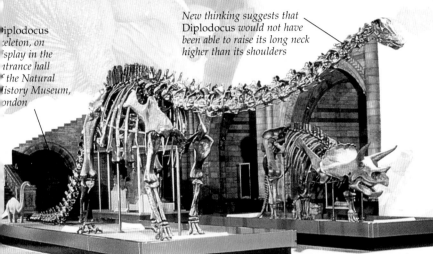

Diplodocus skeleton, on display in the entrance hall of the Natural History Museum, London

New thinking suggests that Diplodocus would not have been able to raise its long neck higher than its shoulders

VISIT A MUSEUM
Dinosaurs are often the most popular exhibits in natural history museums. Collections usually include full-size reconstructions to give people an impression of how dinosaurs might have looked when they were alive. Some museums have computer-animated models with sound effects and realistic movements. Look out, too, for traveling exhibitions from other museums, giving you the opportunity to see dinosaurs discovered in different parts of the world.

FIELD MUSEUM OF NATURAL HISTORY
Chicago, Illinois
www.fmnh.org
The museum has exhibits covering 3.8 billion years of life on Earth and includes:
• "Sue," the world's largest and best-preserved *Tyrannosaurus*
• Remains of some early dinosaurs discovered in Madagascar, which may be older than *Herrerasaurus* and *Eoraptor.*

USEFUL WEB SITES

• Plenty of facts for serious dinosaur enthusiasts:
  www.dinodata.net
• General, award-winning site, with a discussion group:
  www.dinosauria.com
• The American Museum of Natural History's site, with games, activities, and informative interviews:
  www.ology.amnh.org/paleontology/
• For a virtual tour of the dinosaur galleries at the Smithsonian National Museum of Natural History:
  www.nmnh.si.edu/paleo/dino/
• Animated clips of dinosaurs in motion and a dino-finder by zip code:
  dsc.discovery.com/guides/dinosaur/dinosaur/html

Sue's mouth was filled with long, pointed teeth; she may also have suffered from a bad toothache—five holes in her lower jaw are thought to be places of infection.

SMITHSONIAN MUSEUM OF NATURAL HISTORY
Washington, D.C.
www.mnh.si.edu
This is one of the largest collections in the United States and contains:
• dioramas recreating scenes from the Jurassic and Cretaceous periods
• a discovery room where visitors can handle fossils and arrange to watch scientists working in the Fossil Laboratory.

SEE "SUE"
"Sue" is the name given to the largest and most complete skeleton of a tyrannosaur ever discovered. It was found by Sue Hendrickson in 1990, and bought by the Chicago Field Museum. "Sue" went on display in 2000. Except for the skull, the skeleton on display is the real thing (not a plaster cast or plastic model). The bones were so well-preserved, you can see fine details where soft tissue, such as muscles or tendons, were attached.

DINOSAUR NATIONAL MONUMENT QUARRY
Utah
www.nps.gov/dino/dinos.htm
On the site where some of the largest finds from the Jurassic Period have been discovered, visitors can:
• watch scientists at work in the field
• see displays of North American dinosaurs, including long-neck, plant-eating sauropods
• visit a sandstone cliff in which over 1,600 bones have been exposed.

Glossary

ALLOSAUR ("strange lizard") Primitive tetanuran theropod (large meat-eating dinosaur)

AMMONITE One of an extinct group of cephalopods with a coiled, chambered shell that lived in Mesozoic seas

AMPHIBIAN Cold-blooded vertebrate originating in the Carboniferous Period, whose young use gills to breathe during the early stages of life. Living amphibians include frogs, newts, and salamanders.

ANKYLOSAUR ("fused lizard") Four-legged, armored, plant-eating, ornithischian dinosaur with bony plates covering the neck, shoulders, and back, and a horny beak used for cropping plants

AVES Birds, which probably evolved from theropod dinosaurs in the Late Jurassic Period. Some scientists only use "Aves" for modern birds, calling the most primitive birds "Avialae."

BIPEDAL Walking on two hindlimbs, rather than on all fours

BRACHIOPOD Marine invertebrate with a two-valved shell, which evolved in the Cambrian Period

CARNIVORE Meat-eating mammal with sharp teeth, such as a cat, dog, bear, or one of their relatives and ancestors; sometimes used to describe all meat-eating animals

CARNOSAUR Large meat-eating dinosaur with a big skull and teeth. The name was once used for all such theropods but is now restricted to *Allosaurus* and its relatives.

Hadrosaur (*Corythosaurus*)

CEPHALOPOD Marine mollusk with large eyes and well-developed head ringed by tentacles, such as an octopus, squid, or cuttlefish

CERATOPIAN or CERATOPSIAN ("horned face") Bipedal and quadrupedal plant-eating ornithischian dinosaur, with a deep beak and a bony frill at the back of its skull

CERATOSAUR ("horned lizard") One of two major groups of theropods

COLD-BLOODED Depending upon the heat from the sun for body warmth (*see also* WARM-BLOODED)

CONIFER Tree that bears cones, such as a pine or fir

COPROLITE
Fossilized dung

Fossil of a plesiosaur flipper

CRETACEOUS PERIOD Third period of the Mesozoic Era, 145–65 million years ago

CYCAD Palm-like, seed-bearing plant with long fern-like leaves

DIPLODOCID ("double beam") Plant-eating sauropod; one of a family of huge saurischian dinosaurs with long necks and long tails

DROMAEOSAURID ("running lizard") Bird-like, bipedal, carnivorous dinosaur

DUCKBILLED DINOSAUR (*see* HADROSAUR)

EMBRYO Plant or unborn animal in an early stage of development

EVOLUTION The process by which one species gives rise to another. Evolution occurs when individual organisms pass on mutations (chance changes in genes controlling body size, shape, color, and so on). Individuals with beneficial mutations pass them on. Their kind multiplies, and new species arise.

Ginkgo

EXTINCTION The dying-out of a plant or animal species

FOSSIL The remains of something that once lived, preserved in rock. Teeth and bones are more likely to form fossils than softer body parts, such as internal organs.

GASTROLITH Stones swallowed by some animals, such as sauropods, to help grind up food in the stomach

GENUS (plural, GENERA) Group of related organisms, ranked between the levels of family and species

GINKGO Deciduous tree that grows to around 115 ft (25 m) in height, which evolved in the Triassic Period and survives essentially unchanged to this day

HADROSAUR ("bulky lizard") Duck-billed dinosaur; large, bipedal/quadrupedal ornithopod from the Late Cretaceous Period with a duck-like beak used for browsing on vegetation

HERBIVORE Animal that feeds on plants

IGUANODONTIAN ("Iguana teeth") Large, bipedal/quadrupedal plant-eating ornithopod from the Early Cretaceous Period (*see also* ORNITHOPOD)

INVERTEBRATE Animal without a backbone

JURASSIC Second period of the Mesozoic Era, 200–145 million years ago

MAMMAL Warm-blooded, hairy vertebrate that suckles its young

MANIRAPTORAN ("grasping hands") Tetanuran theropod with long arms and hands, including predatory dinosaurs, such as *Velociraptor*, and birds

MEGALOSAUR ("great lizard") Primitive tetanuran theropod, less advanced than an allosaur

MESOZOIC "Middle life" geological era about 250–65 million years ago, containing the Triassic, Jurassic, and Cretaceous periods; the "Age of the Dinosaurs." Dinosaurs became extinct at the end of the era.

ORNITHISCHIAN ("bird hips") One of two main dinosaur groups. In ornithischian dinosaurs the pelvis is similar to that of birds. (see also SAURISCHIAN)

ORNITHOPOD ("bird feet") Bipedal ornithischian dinosaur with long hindlimbs

OVIRAPTORID ("egg stealer") Maniraptoran theropod dinosaur with a beak and long legs

PACHYCEPHALOSAUR ("thick-headed lizard") Bipedal ornithischian dinosaur with a thick skull

Cycad

PALEONTOLOGIST Someone who studies paleontology

PALEONTOLOGY The scientific study of fossilized plants and animals

PALEOZOIC "Ancient life" geological era from 540–240 million years ago, containing the Cambrian, Ordovician, Silurian, Devonian, Carboniferous, and Permian periods

PLESIOSAUR Large Mesozoic marine reptile with flipper-shaped limbs and (often) a long neck

PREDATOR Animal or plant that preys on animals for food

PRESERVATION Keeping something (such as a fossil) free from harm or decay

PROSAUROPOD Early plant-eating saurischian dinosaur that lived from the Late Triassic to Early Jurassic eras

PSITTACOSAUR ("parrot lizard") Ceratopian ornithischian plant-eater from the Cretaceous Period. A psittacosaur was bipedal with a deep, parrot-like beak.

PTEROSAUR ("winged lizard") Flying reptile of the Mesozoic Era, related to the dinosaurs

QUADRUPEDAL Walking on all fours

REPTILE Cold-blooded, scaly vertebrate that reproduces by laying eggs or giving birth on land. Living reptiles include lizards, snakes, turtles, and crocodiles.

SAURISCHIAN ("lizard hips") One of two main dinosaur groups. In saurischian dinosaurs, the pelvis is similar to that of lizards. (see also ORNITHISCHIAN)

SAUROPOD ("lizard feet") Huge, plant-eating quadrupedal saurischian dinosaur that lived through most of the Mesozoic Era

SAUROPODOMORPH ("lizard foot form") Large plant-eating quadrupedal saurischian dinosaur, including the prosauropods and sauropods

SCUTE Bony plate with a horny covering set into an animal's skin to protect it from an enemy's teeth and claws

SEDIMENT Material deposited by wind, water, or ice

SKULL The head's bony framework protecting the brain, eyes, ears, and nasal passages

SPECIES The level below genus in the classification of living things. Individuals in a species can breed to produce fertile young.

STEGOSAUR ("plated/roofed lizard") Plant-eating, quadrupedal ornithischian dinosaur with two tall rows of bony plates running down its neck, back, and tail

TETANURAN ("stiff tail") One of the two main groups of theropod dinosaurs

THECODONT ("socket teeth") One of a mixed group of archosaurs that includes dinosaurs, crocodiles, and pterosaurs

THEROPOD ("beast feet") One of a group of predatory dinosaurs with sharp teeth and claws

TITANOSAUR ("gigantic lizard") Huge, quadrupedal plant-eating sauropod

TRACE FOSSIL Trace left by a prehistoric creature, such as its footprints, eggs, bite marks, droppings, and fossil impressions of skin, hair, and feathers

TRIASSIC First period of the Mesozoic Era, about 250–200 million years ago

Dromaeosaurid (*Velociraptor*)

TYRANNOSAURID ("tyrant lizard") Huge, bipedal carnivorous tetanuran theropod characterized by a large head, short arms, two-fingered hands, and massive hindlimbs; flourished during the Late Cretaceous Period in North America and Asia

WARM-BLOODED Keeping body temperature at a constant level, often above or below that of the surrounding environment, by turning energy from food into heat (see also COLD-BLOODED)

Tyrannosaurid (*Tyrannosaurus*)

Index

Acknowledgments

The publisher would like to thank:
Angela Milner and the staff of the British Museum (Natural History); Kew Gardens and Clifton Nurseries for advice and plant specimens for photography; Trevor Smith's Animal World; The Institute of Vertebrate Palaeoanthropology, Beijing, for permission to photograph Chinese dinosaurs; Brian Carter for obtaining plant specimens; Victoria Sorzano for typing; William Lindsay for advice on pp 52-53 and pp 54-55; Fred Ford and Mike Pilley of Radius Graphics; Jane Parker for the index; Richard Czapnik for design assistance; and Dave King for special photography on pp 6-7 and pp 10-11.

Picture credits
t=top, b=bottom, m=middle, l=left, r=right

American Museum of Natural History: 44bl, 54tl; /C. Chesak 42bl;
ANT/NHPA: 7tr;
Artia Foreign Trade Corporation: /Zdenek Burian 10m;
BBC Hulton Picture Library: 8tl, 9tm, 31t;
Booth Museum of Natural History: 50b;
The Bridgeman Art Library: 17bl;
The British Museum (Natural History): 52tl, 52ml, 55tr;
Bruce Coleman Ltd: 14-15; /Jane Burton 6ml, 13br, 29ml, 35tl, 36tl, 39tr, 50tl, 57bl, 59tl; /Jules Cowan 51br; /Janos Jurka 34tl;
Corbis: 69b; /James L. Amos 68mr; /Tom Bean 64-65; /Derek Hall/Frank Lane Picture Agency 68tl;
Albert Dickson: 46bl;
Alistair Duncan: 71ml;
Robert Harding: 63tr;
The Illustrated London News: 46tl;
The Image Bank: /L. Castaneda 15mr;

Kobal Collection: 63m; *Jurassic Park III* © ILM (Industrial Light & Magic) 68bl;
The Mansell Collection: 28tl, 42mr, 56tr;
Mary Evans Picture Library: 9bl, 9m, 12tl, 16bl, 25ml, 34ml, 35bm, 62tl, 62bl, 62mr;
Museo Arentino De Cirendas Naterales, Buenos Aires: 64bl;
The Natural History Museum, London: 23bl, 64tl, 65tm, 68-69;
Natural Science Photos: /Arthur Hayward 24tr, 29bl, 37tr; /G. Kinns 30tl; /C.A. Walker 40tl;
David Norman: 53mr;
Planet Earth Pictures: /Richard Beales 32tl; /Ken Lucas 31mr;
Rex Features: 66-67, 69m; /Simon Runtin 68br;
Royal Tyrrel Museum, Canada: 66mr, 70-71;
Science Photo Library: /David A. Hardy 49tl; /Philippe Plailly/Eurelios 65ml, 69t;
The South Florida Museum of Natural History: 51tr, 51cr.

Picture research: Angela Murphy, Celia Dearing

Illustrations by:
Bedrock: 12m, 14tl;
Angelika Elsebach: 21tl, 36b;
Sandie Hill: 20br, 28tr, 44tr;
Mark Iley: 18bl;
Malcolm McGregor: 43bl;
Richard Ward: 26bm, 47b;
Ann Winterbotham: 10tl;
John Woodcock: 6tr, 7mr, 14b, 14ml

Cover images:
Front: Ron Watts/Corbis, b

All other images © Dorling Kindersley
For more information see **www.dkimages.com**